Christ
Buil(

*I'll take your part
When darkness comes
And pain is all around
Like a bridge over troubled water*

*To Jim
A partner in the cause,
Very best of wishes
Marcus*

Marcus Braybrooke

Christians and Jews Building Bridges

*To our many friends mentioned in the book
who have enriched Mary's and my life
by their friendship
and strengthened our faith in God,
whose love no evil can defeat*

'A friend loveth at all times...and sticketh closer than a brother or sister.'

The rights of Marcus Braybrooke as author have been asserted in accordance with the Copyrights, Designs and Patents Act 1998

© Marcus Braybrooke 2012

ISBN 978-1-291-37948-8

Braybrooke Press

Christians and Jews Building Bridges

The seventieth anniversary of the founding of the Council of Christians and Jews in Britain is a good time to take a look at Christian-Jewish relations today.

The first part of this book looks back at the issues which have been of most importance in the last twenty years and will, I hope, be a useful survey for all who are concerned for understanding and co-operation between the two faith communities. This is a personal reflection and not an official history of the Council of Christians and Jews (CCJ), although the Council is centre stage.

The second part looks at some of the people who have been most active in this field. It is also a reminder that dialogue does not take place between religions but between people.

For those who want the whole story of CCJ, I refer them back to my earlier book, *Children of One God,* which told the story of the first fifty years of the Council of Christian and Jews

Christians and Jews Building Bridges

CONTENTS

Section One: The Issues

1 Yesterday's Agenda? What on earth is CCJ for?
2 Education: Informing and Changing Perceptions:
3 A New Political Agenda: Encouraging Social Cohesion.
4 The Continuing struggle against Antisemitism
5 The State of Israel: Cause of Misunderstanding
6 Interpreting Israel to an impatient Church
7 Mission
8 Catholic-Jewish Relations
9 Wider Links

Section Two: The People

10 Local Branches More about People than Theology.
11 At the Centre (1): Outstanding Leaders
12 At the Centre (2): Dedicated Staff
13 'The Souls of the Righteous are in the hand of God'
14 Together for the Future

Section One: The Issues

Chapter 1 Yesterday's Agenda? What on earth is CCJ for?

It is not incumbent upon you to complete the work, but neither are you at liberty to desist from it. Rabbi Tarfon

Why should the 70th Anniversary of The Council of Christians and Jews, be a time for regret? Perhaps because its work is as necessary today as it was when the CCJ was formed in 1942. In those dark days of the Second World War, news of the Nazi's murderous attacks on Jews was beginning to reach Britain. One might have hoped that by now antisemitism had been eradicated. Sadly, although the situation today is very different, antisemitism, which is forever adopting different disguises and finding fresh excuses for its resurgence, is as real a danger as ever.

Dispelling centuries-old prejudice and ignorance requires long and persistent educational programmes. There are no instant successes to catch the headlines. When a potential donor asked James Parkes (1896-1981), who dedicated his life to securing a 'fair deal for the Jews,' 'How long will it take to get rid of antisemitism?' He replied, 'Three hundred years.' The donor answered, 'If you had said anything less, I would not give you any money.' Possibly even sadder is the fact that the theological task to which Parkes devoted his life is by no means complete. Nonetheless, the past antagonism of Christians to Jews and Judaism has been replaced to a large extent by genuine appreciation.

Antisemitism, even so, remains a present threat. On the occasion of the 50th Anniversary, George Carey, the then Archbishop of Canterbury, spoke of the 'intolerance, antisemitism, xenophobia and downright jealousy and envy,' which still haunted the face of Europe. Chief Rabbi Jonathan Sacks took as the title of his address 'Every Fifty Years, We Must Begin Again.' The same is probably true today. In January 2009, antisemitic attacks in Great Britain reached their highest point since record-keeping began. The same was true for Europe as a whole, where antisemitic attacks were up three hundred per cent over the previous year.

There is, therefore, still a great deal to do. However the most cursory of reflections will reveal the huge headway that has been made over the last 70 years. There has been a revolutionary change in the official teaching of the Churches about Jews and Judaism. Jesus is now seen as a 'faithful Jew'. The evil accusation that in killing Jesus 'the Jews' were guilty of 'deicide', has been completely repudiated by the Churches. Church statements now routinely affirm that God's covenant with the Jewish people is everlasting and recognise that Judaism is still today a spiritually vibrant religion. No wonder Gerald Priestland, who was the BBC religious affairs correspondent in the 1980s, could say that the change in Jewish-Christian relations was one of the few pieces of good religious news that he was able to report. This teaching, however, still needs to be much better known by clergy and rabbis, in local Jewish and Christian faith communities, and by the wider public.

CCJ cannot take all the credit for these changes, but without CCJ they would not have happened. Instead of becoming widely known by the faithful and indeed being recognised by the leaders of British society and by the press, these changes would have been – and could still be - confined to scholarly footnotes. Moreover, CCJ's influence has spread far beyond Britain, because its example has been copied in many other countries.

Antisemitism takes many forms. The work, therefore, of CCJ is multi-faceted and constantly changing, and not easily reduced to a couple of sound bites.

Writing of the early years of CCJ, Jan Fuchs said, 'CCJ has to be a jack-of-all trades, catering for large formal gatherings, more intimate house meetings, for conferences and seminars where people live, pray, celebrate and talk together. The spill-off from learning and intellectual stimulation is often the personal friendship which develops. People show open joy when they meet again year after year. CCJ has to cater for those at the centre of activities and those on the periphery, those who are satisfied with co-existence and tolerance and those who crave for dialogue and human nearness. Compared with congregational life, there are Christmas Christians and Yom Kippur Jews (only once a year!). There are the ones in charge (the 'Marchers') and the followers, the occasionals and the regulars, the quiet thinker, and the one who always does the jobs that nobody else wants to do. CCJ needs all of them as much as church and synagogue does and it needs their membership fees in order to function.'

It is said that David Ben-Gurion, Israel's first Prime Minister, asked countless Jewish figures across the world for their definition of 'Who is a Jew?' The answers were so different that Ben Gurion gave up. It is tempting to do the same in describing the work of CCJ. Its work is so varied that different people's perceptions of it are equally varied.

'What is CCJ for?' is a recurring topic of discussion at CCJ trustees meetings.

In part this is because of the urgent and ever recurring need to assess the state of Jewish–Christian relationships. Anti-semitism and xenophobia are still too much in evidence, despite theological advances.

Additionally, potential donors have to be convinced that CCJ deserves their support in an environment where there are countless good causes. The pluralist, multifaith context in which CCJ works is ever changing. CCJ's work is therefore, constantly changing, to ensure the continuing relevance of its work.

On one occasion, members of the Trustees were asked to sum up CCJ in eight words. Here are some of their attempts:

> Educate, enrich, bringing together Jews and Christians.
>
> Personal friendships and community building.
>
> Faith to faith – through dialogue.
>
> To fight racism and create harmony.
>
> Jews and Christians meeting in friendship and dialogue.
>
> Break down barriers and prevent unfortunate misunderstandings.

> To bridge the gap, to unite the voices.
>
> To build trust and understanding between religions.
>
> Dialogue, reconciliation and understanding between cultures.
>
> Promote understanding between people of different faiths.
>
> To promote love of each other with understanding.
>
> Overcome misunderstanding between different faiths.

In 2003 there was a long discussion at the Executive Committee about CCJ's image. Paul Winner, a long time and faithful member of CCJ, said that at the highest level 'CCJ provides a forum for discussion and dialogue.' There was, however, confusion about what CCJ could achieve. 'It cannot influence everything and everyone – but clergy and opinion-formers are important.' Revd Adrian Robbins-Cole wondered whether for some clergy Christian-Jewish dialogue was seen as yesterday's issue and that they were more interested in relations with Muslims. It was recognised that the role of branches was important but different from national concerns. The value of work with young people was highlighted. It was also suggested CCJ should have more input in Continued Ministerial Training of Anglican clergy.

Flash Back

The formal announcement of the establishment of the Council of Christians and Jews was made on October 1st, 1942. The beginnings, however, date back to November 19th 1941, when Archbishop of Canterbury William Temple and the Chief Rabbi Dr J.H Hertz met for lunch. They got on splendidly. They agreed that a Christian–Jewish Council was needed. Its task would be to resist and dispel all forms of prejudice, especially antisemitism, and to affirm the shared ethical teachings of the two religions which were the basis of Western civilization that was under serious threat in the time of war. The then Chief Rabbi, Dr J H Hertz said, 'National life, religion, and civilization all depended on the attitude of any society to the Jew.'

After the war CCJ concentrated on its educational work of helping Christians - both at school and in church – to appreciate Judaism and to meet and get to know Jews.

It was not until the 1960s, after nearly twenty years of silence, that the horrors of the Holocaust became a subject of public discourse. Slowly, spurred on by the Second Vatican Council's decree *Nostra Aetate*, Christians began to recognise and correct the long history of anti-Jewish teaching that had contributed so much to the sufferings of the Jews. By the 1980s, making this theological revolution known to clergy and church members became an additional and unfinished task for CCJ.

By the eighties, however, the changing situation in Israel made some Christians less sympathetic to the work of CCJ, because there was a tendency, unfairly, to blame Jews in

Britain for the harsh measures of the Israeli Likud government. By the eighties Israel was no longer seen as the 'under-dog.' Settlements in the West Bank and Gaza made a 'Land for Peace' agreement less likely. Repressive measures in the West Bank were condemned by some senior Israeli reserve officers, one of whom said, 'we are gradually losing our humanity.' The invasion of Lebanon and the siege of Beirut - intended to drive the Palestinian Liberation Army from the city - was watched on television by millions across the world. As the historian Martin Gilbert has written, 'The daily television transmission of Israeli artillery bombarding Beirut, the columns of smoke, dust and fire rising in the air, and close-up pictures of destruction, including on one occasion serious damage to a hospital, caused immense harm to Israel's international image, and much anguished discussion within Israel itself.' Worse was to come with the massacre of over 2,000 Palestinian men, women and children in the refugee camps of Sabra and Chatila which 'shocked the world.'

The unpopularity in Britain of Israeli government actions has continued to create real challenges for the CCJ. As we shall see, CCJ has always given support to those working for reconciliation and peace in Israel-Palestine, but it has also vigorously and consistently resisted the exploitation of public hostility to Israel by antisemites. It has also helped people in Britain to gain a more balanced view of the situation. Since the nineties educational tours to Israel have become an important feature of CCJ's programme.

In the nineties, because of the conflicts in former Yugoslavia, some prophetic voices began to warn of the danger of religiously-motivated violence. The mood, however, as the Millennium approached was optimistic. Many religious leaders shared the vision of a 'Global Ethic', which had been proclaimed at the 1993 Parliament of World Religions in Chicago, as a contribution to a more just and peaceful world. Christians and Jews with members of other faiths emphasised the ethical values that they shared and their common concern for peace, human rights, the relief of poverty and the protection of the environment.

In the book *Yes to a Global Ethic*, Archbishop George Carey, wrote, 'The vision behind the Declaration of the Religions for a Global Ethic is twofold: the fundamental unity of the human family and the potential of all faiths to make a distinctive contribution toward world peace. This is something to celebrate. I believe that we are at a moment in world history when men and women of good will can make an unparalleled contribution towards peace among the nations. We who are leaders must set the pace. We must with integrity seek a true tolerance based upon a commitment to each other and espouse policies which will transcend all forms of behaviour that create hatred, resentment and division.' Chief Rabbi Jonathan Sacks highlighted the contribution that Judaism could make to this emerging Global Ethic. Judaism 'is the guardian of an ancient but still compelling dream. To heal where others harm, mend where others destroy, to redeem evil by turning its energies to good. He called upon the faithful to become co-authors with God of the world that ought to be.'

There was also optimism about the possibility of a peace settlement between Israelis and Palestinians. André Chouraqui, a writer and translator, spoke of the moves towards peace in the Middle East as 'pointing to an era of peace between three religions which, rooted in the same Biblical culture, proclaim the same God and essentially the same ethic of Torah, Gospel and Qu'ran. The modern echo of this ethic can be found in the aspirations of the 1948 Universal Declaration of Human Rights and more recently in the Declaration of a Global Ethic of the Parliament of the World's Religions, which has revived the great ideals of brotherhood, peace, union between different ethnic groups, peoples, nations, churches.'

This moment of hope was soon shattered by '9/11,' - the attack on the Twin Towers in New York - and by the turbulence that followed it. The dangers of extremism and religiously motivated violence became clear for all to see. Jews and Christians were united in their opposition to religiously motivated extremism from any source. Concern was increased by the fact that the subsequent London bombings were carried out by British citizens. The context in which CCJ was now called to operate had changed dramatically. CCJ brought its long experience of inter-communal work to the urgent task of healing the divisions in British society, which were often reinforced by religious differences.

The so-called 'War against Terrorism', the invasion of Afghanistan and of Iraq and growing turbulence in the Middle East was accompanied by a rapid rise of antisemitism, as well as Islamaphobia, in Britain and across Western Europe. In some quarters Israel rather than the terrorists was blamed for the rise in violence and conflict. Jewish students found themselves subject to attack on campuses and antisemitism and racism has continued to increase. 'In five weeks in January 2009, in London alone,

220 anti-Semitic incidents were recorded by the police' wrote the Chief Rabbi Lord Sacks,' Worshippers on their way to the synagogue at which I pray were shouted at by a passer-by with the words, "Hitler should have finished the job."'

The dangers of the new century have made the work of CCJ as important as ever, although other difficulties have created problems. The influence on society of both Judaism and Christianity has been declining as the membership of both church and synagogue has fallen. Attention has also switched to the relationship of both Judaism and Christianity to Islam, although CCJ maintained its focus on Jewish-Christian relations. More recently Jewish and Christian leaders have become increasingly aware of the danger to society of aggressive secularism, which seeks to exclude religion from public life.

These changes have meant that CCJ's work has again focussed on education and building constructive relations between all members of the Jewish and Christian communities. CCJ continues to be active in promoting information and knowledge, which is enriching in its own right, as well as part of the fight against antisemitism and xenophobia in times of economic challenge and social and political change. It has also meant that the work of local CCJ branches has taken on a new importance.

Chapter 2   Education:
Informing and Changing Perceptions:

The underlying causes of the modern Jewish problem are to be found in the past failure of the Christian community either to understand or do justice to the Jews.

Revd W.W. Simpson, first General Secretary of CCJ

Education is central to the work of the CCJ. It has to be long-term and persistent. It is also very varied - involving work in schools, the production of educational material, work with students, courses for clergy and rabbis and those in training, talks to congregations, and articles for a variety of journals and newsletters.

The Changing Contexts for CCJ's Educational Work

Soon after CCJ's establishment, the 1944 (Butler) Education Act, which required Religious Instruction in all Local Authority schools, was passed. In 1949, when Albert Polack - a former house master at Clifton College, Bristol, - became CCJ Education Officer, Christians then might have been familiar with the Old Testament, but knew hardly anything about Rabbinic or contemporary Judaism. It was hoped that learning more about Jews and Judaism would dispel prejudice. Albert Polack spent much of his time giving talks to schools and other audiences.

CCJ's pioneering educational material was at that time unique. Its 'One God - The Ways He is Worshipped and Served'- was a series of four filmstrips. A booklet on 'Tolerance – Can it be Taught?' - was published to show what Jews and Christians have in common. In 1955, as a result of a survey of history textbooks, a booklet called 'History without Bias' was produced, which amongst other things questioned the use as a set book of 'The Prioress' tale' from Chaucer's Canterbury Tales. There seems to have been little attention to helping Jewish children learn more about Christianity – probably because it was assumed that all Christians would try to win converts.

By the early sixties some members of CCJ and of the World Congress of Faiths were arguing that children should learn a little about all religions, if they were to understand the world in which they were growing up. In the pioneering spirit of breaking new ground, which is still characteristic of much of CCJ's work, Bernard Cousins, an active member of CCJ, wrote a memorandum on this subject as early as 1959, followed by a booklet 'Introducing Children to World Religions' in 1966.

In the 1970s RI became RE. Religious Instruction (R.I.) was intended to help children become good Christians ('nurture'), although Jewish parents could withdraw their children from these classes. Religious Education (R.E.) was justified on the grounds that children could not understand the present or the past without knowledge of religion. Increasingly RE was expected to include some study of world religions. Several members of CCJ helped to shape the agreed syllabi. Judaism because of its many visual aids has been a popular choice for teachers. CCJ provided teachers with artefacts, produced educational material, including the slide-tape programmes *Living Judaism* and *In Good Faith*. A series of excellent educational supplements were published with *Common Ground*. CCJ local activists gave many talks to primary children about Jewish and Christian festivals and rabbis gave generously of their time to show school parties round their synagogue – and still do.

In the 1980s, CCJ started to give special attention to making clergy and rabbis aware of the far-reaching changes taking place, at a scholarly level, in Christian teaching about Judaism. At that time the journal *Theology* still classified any book on Judaism under the heading 'Old Testament.' Even as late as 1986 Dr Alistair Hunter in a Waley Cohen lecture could surprise a CCJ audience by saying that the recognition by Christian and Jewish scholars that Jesus was a faithful Jew was a 'minor revolution in Biblical studies' with 'more far-reaching consequences than is generally recognised.'

CCJ took the lead in making the fruits of this 'minor revolution' known in many journal articles, magazine features and lectures. Two land-mark conferences on 'The Parting of the Ways' were arranged by CCJ and Birmingham's Centre for the Study of Judaism and Jewish-Christian Relations - led by Rabbi Dr Norman Solomon - at Selly Oak. These showed that Christianity did not displace Judaism, but that both Rabbinic Judaism and the Christian Church were creative responses to the shared heritage of the Hebrew Bible.

By the late 1980s and 1990s this new theological scholarship which has transformed Christian understanding of Judaism began to be acknowledged in statements made by most mainline Churches. The Vatican issued a number of documents to amplify the teaching of *Nostra Aetate*, which had started this rethinking in the Roman Catholic Church nearly two decades earlier. In 1985, the Church of Scotland issued two reports. One was on *Jews and Christians Today* and the other was on *Antisemitism in the World Today*. In 1988 the Lambeth Conference of Anglican bishops from across the world commended the document *Jews, Christians and Muslims*, which remains, in effect, the only authoritative Anglican statement on the subject. It would not have been agreed without the tireless work of the Bishop of Oxford Richard Harries, who was soon to become chairman of CCJ.

In the 1990s, rightly responding to the extent to which Judaism was now part of the national schools' curriculum, something of a paradigm shift occurred in the strategic thinking of CCJ. A Position Paper suggested their focus should now be on adults who were likely to be in a position to influence others, including the young. The paper pointed out that CCJ's work should 'reflect our concern with personal and communal reconciliation.' Recognising the importance of academic study the paper affirmed 'our work is distinguished by its emphasis on individual student responses to the material presented.'

Six aims were identified:

1. To ensure that present and future RE teachers and clergy (etc.)... have a sympathetic and informed understanding of Judaism, the contemporary Jewish community, and Jewish-Christian relations.

2. To promote an understanding of Christian-Jewish

relations in the Christian and Jewish communities.

3. To clarify the religious and ethical aims of teaching the Holocaust and to provide guidance for such teaching.

4. To enrich the educational content of CCJ branches.

5. To promote an informed Christian understanding of contemporary Israel.

6. To promote Jewish-Christian contributions to appropriate social issues.

Writing in the 1990s, the journalist and broadcaster Laurence Spicer gave this description of the core activity of CCJ: 'Sister Margaret Shepherd and Jonathan Gorsky, cross the country leading courses and holding seminars in universities and schools. At least two fresh booklets are issued each year to add to the specialist publications on Jews and Christians. Only by instilling knowledge, understanding and respect can we look forward to a peaceful future. That is the task of CCJ.'

There is, however, no substitute for meeting members of another faith - thus from the very beginning CCJ, as we shall see, has put great emphasis on building up a network of local branches, where relationships can be fostered and the dialogue for which CCJ is well known can take place.

Laurence Spicer also highlighted the Young Leadership programme. CCJ has given particular attention to work with Young Adults. There have been a number of tours to Israel for Young Adults described later. In 1993, however, a group of Young Leaders went to Rome and had the privilege of being received by the Pope in a private audience. In an address to the Pope, Andrew White – now Vicar of Baghdad emphasised the importance of the next generation taking part in Christian-Jewish dialogue. In reply the Pope said that 'it was fitting that young Christians and Jews should be united in such a great task.'

'From Theology to Action' was the theme for The Young Leadership Conference in 1995. The emphasis was on what practical steps could be taken to improve community relations. The speakers were Rabbi Boteach, who had founded the Oxford University Le Chaim Society, which had more than 1,000 members, and Revd Kenneth Leech, who had been Director of the Runnymede Trust.

CCJ played an active part in preparing material for the UK's first Holocaust Memorial Day, on January 27th, 2001. It is a role it still continues today, working with its partner Churches Together in Britain and Ireland (CTBI) to ensure that Holocaust Memorial Day materials are made available to all UK Christian clergy. The excellent publication *The Holocaust: Faith, Morality and Ethics* edited by Jane Clements, Jonathan Gorsky and Rosie Boston, has been widely used and valued by teachers.

By the beginning of the 21st century the situation was once more changing. Relations with Islam became a public priority. Yet at the same time some academic institutions began to offer courses on Jewish-Christian relations.

Jewish-Christian Relations are still important

Jane Clements, one time CCJ Education Officer, said of the early years of the new century that 'the recognised importance of Jewish-Christian relations declined to its nadir. The received wisdom in the religious world was that this was a relationship which had been immensely destructive but that, since 1945, Christians had set about their own education and wounds had largely healed. Repeatedly, throughout my time at CCJ, I was told that "Christian-Jewish relations are *passé*; relations with Islam are what really matters."'

The attack on the Twin Towers in 2001 and the London bombings reinforced the attention to Islam.

Two Young Leadership conferences were held in 2001: one was on 'About Time: Christians and Jews in the New Century,' and the other on 'Who's Listening: Does Dialogue have any value post-September 11th?' To show that CCJ is not all about words, in 2002 Gemma Abbs, CCJ's Youth Officer took a group of young people to the Czech Republic to restore a Jewish cemetery, which the small ageing Jewish community was itself unable to look after. Later the group helped to renovate the garden of a Salvation Army Homeless Drop-in centre in King's Cross.

It is to the great credit of CCJ that, in these more difficult times, Christian-Jewish relations were not ignored. They have their own specific dynamics – just as does the dialogue of Christians and Muslims, of Jews and Muslims, of members of the three faiths together and of multi-faith dialogue. CCJ, under the leadership of Margaret Shepherd remained firmly focussed on the bilateral dialogue between Jews and Christians. 'The fact that CCJ did endure' in Jane Clements' words, 'says a lot for those who recognised that the engagement with "the other" for the sake of heaven is a profitable pursuit. Jews and Christians in dialogue have learnt to say the unpalatable to each other and to be critical friends. We have not simply continued to explore texts together, but now understand that we do so using different language and from contrasting traditions. Yet we can also acknowledge that this only serves to underline the richness and diversity of the Divine.' There was, therefore, real progress in the dialogue among those deeply involved in it - even if the wider church seemed less interested.

Scholarly Dialogue

Evidence of the growth of scholarly dialogue is shown by the growing number of academic institutions which offer courses in Jewish-Christian relations.

There were already various academic courses and centres for Biblical studies and the study of Judaism. The Oxford Centre for Hebrew and Jewish Studies was founded in 1972 by Dr David Patterson, who was its President until his retirement in 1992. The Centre was originally based at the Oriental Institute in Pusey Lane, Oxford, later moving in 1973 to rented premises at 45 St Giles. At the same time the Centre acquired, thanks to the generosity of the Charles Wolfson Charitable Trust, the use of Yarnton Manor, an early seventeenth-century house and rural estate just outside Oxford. In 1991 another donor enabled the Centre to purchase the property. Integration with the University was accomplished in the autumn of 2000, with the formation of the Oxford University Teaching and Research Unit in Hebrew and Jewish Studies. Its work includes Jewish history, Talmudic studies and now Jewish-Islamic and Jewish-Christian relations at all periods of their histories.

The University of Manchester has a long and distinguished record in the research and teaching of Jewish studies, boasting such eminent scholars as Alexander Altmann, James Barr, Edward Ullendorf and Meir Wallenstein. The Centre for Jewish studies was established when the existing provision was strengthened by the creation of the Alliance chair in Modern Jewish Studies. In 1997 Professor Bernard Jackson was appointed to the chair and became co-director with Professor Philip Alexander. In 2009, Professor Jackson retired and was succeeded as co-director by Professor Alexander Samely. In 2011 Professor Alexander retired and was succeeded as co-director by Professor Danile Langton.

Thanks in part to CCJ's work, both 'Jewish-Christian Relations' and 'Interfaith Dialogue' were becoming academic subjects in their own right. The pioneering work of Rabbi Dr Norman Solomon at The Centre for the Study of Judaism and Jewish Christian Relations at the Selly Oak Colleges in Birmingham has already been mentioned. Interfaith dialogue has been a priority of The Sternberg Centre for Judaism. The Centre, in London, is a campus hosting a number of Jewish institutions, built around the 18th-century Finchley manor house. The centre was opened in 1981 by the Manor House Trust and is now named after Sir Sigmund Sternberg. The founding organisations were Leo Baeck College and the Akiva School. The (Masorti) New North London Synagogue is now also located there. The centre also hosted the Jewish Museum, Finchley until

2007. Some Christians have joined the rabbinic classes at Leo Baeck. The Centre also has a room set aside for interfaith sharing and has hosted many meetings of the Manor House Dialogue Group.

From the early 1990s Westminster College (now part of Oxford Brookes University) included the study of Judaism and Jewish-Christian Relations in some degree and diploma courses. In 1997 Heythrop College in London introduced a Diploma on Christian-Jewish Relations. This was a one-year course, taught on one evening a week. Heythrop now offers a BA in Abrahamic Religions. At Cambridge, The Centre for Jewish Christian Studies led with great energy and enthusiasm by Ed Kessler, was established in 1997. The project received active support and advice from CCJ. It is now part of the Woolf Institute of Abrahamic Faiths,

Other Universities offering related courses include the Centre for Jewish Studies at the University of Leeds; the Centre for Jewish Studies at SOAS, London; the Department of Hebrew and Jewish Studies at University College, London; the London School of Jewish Studies; the Universities of Exeter and Leicester; and University of Wales, at Lampeter.

CCJ has also worked very closely with the Parkes Institute at the University of Southampton. James Parkes, as we have seen, was a pioneer of the Churches' new relationship with Judaism. He collected an enormous amount of material on Christian-Jewish relations, which he transferred to what became known as the Parkes Library at the University of Southampton. Parkes' hope was that the library would become the focal point of an international research and teaching centre on Jewish/ non-Jewish Relations. Some twenty-one years after his death, his vision was realised with the development of the Parkes Institute, headed by Professor Tony Kushner. The Institute covers four areas of activity: the library, research, teaching undergraduates, MA and PhD students and outreach work in co-operation with many organisations within and outside the UK.

The Sisters of Sion, a Roman Catholic order, have for a long time been close partners with CCJ. Sister Margaret Shepherd, a former Director of CCJ, was a member of the Order. Many of the community at Ammerdown, where several conferences have been held, were also Sisters of Sion. The Sion Centre for Dialogue and Encounter has a very important educational role. Its library has over 4,000 books.

Several members of CCJ belong to the London Society of Jews and Christians, which was founded in 1927. The Society seeks to increase religious understanding and to promote goodwill and cooperation between Jews and Christians, with mutual respect for the differences in faith and practice and to combat religious intolerance.

Mention should also be made of the close co-operation of many Jewish organisations with the work of CCJ, especially the Board of Deputies, the Sternberg Centre, the Anglo Israel Association, the London Jewish Cultural Centre and the Jewish Museum.

Unlike academic study, which aims to be objective, dialogue between committed believers has a different dynamic. Participants struggle to hear what God is saying today through their different traditions. In such dialogue, at its deepest, where there is real trust and friendship, 'the partners share their convictions and confront their differences... This springs from the deep conviction of God's activity in the whole of human history and of God's presence within the various religious traditions of humankind.' As the American Reform theologian Rabbi Eugene Borowitz said, such dialogue 'shows its conviction that truth is ultimately one.' It is not sufficient for Jews and Christians to pursue parallel paths without learning from and being changed by the other.

Indeed this is an area that CCJ now has begun to revisit. There is in some quarters a feeling that Christian-Jewish dialogue has 'atrophied' or has 'reached a plateau'. Although there was a particularly important academic seminar in 2001 entitled 'Can Christianity be taught without Supersessionism?' at which both Rowan Williams, at that time still Archbishop of Wales, and Richard Harries, Bishop of Oxford, spoke, the Churches have been reluctant to follow through the theological implications of the new appreciation of Judaism. As Richard Harries says, 'I don't think even now we have begun to bring about that fundamental change in attitudes which is required from teachers of the faith.' In 2011 the CCJ Advisory Board called on the CCJ Trustees to look further at the theology of the Jewish–Christian dialogic encounter. They invited Rabbi Dr Tony Bayfield to call together a group to investigate this area and hopefully lead to theological advances over the next 4 years. The group had its first meeting in March 2012 and its work is progressing.

Chapter 3. A New Political Agenda: Encouraging Social Cohesion.

How wonderful it is, how pleasant, for God's people to live together in harmony. (Psalm 133, 1)

Since 2008 there has been a surprising and alarming increase in antisemitism and racism. It has given a new urgency to the work of CCJ. Although the threat is primarily motivated by religious extremism and by hostility to Israel, rather than by traditional Christian anti-Jewish teaching, correcting anti-Judaism in the churches' teaching and liturgy is still important.

Does the public know Jesus was a Jew?

Many members of the general public are still unaware of the progress in Jewish-Christian relations that has already been made. In 2009 Howard Jacobson – himself a Jew – presented a television programme entitled 'Jesus the Jew.' Writing about this programme Jacobson said, 'Jesus was a Jew. Everyone knows that don't they? Well. It would seem they do and they don't. It is certainly not the view of most Christians, nor is it common knowledge among atheists or even Jews.' If Jacobson is right, CCJ has an enormous continuing task of public education. It may still be true, as Stuart Blanch, former Archbishop of York, said some years ago 'that every church needs a notice over the door to the effect that "Jesus was a Jew" – and perhaps that goes for the synagogue, too.'

It is true that much of the new understanding has been incorporated into New Testament studies at theological colleges and seminaries and so may percolate to the laity. Clergy, however, are all too quick to forget what they have studied when they get into the pulpit. Lord Harries, former chairman of CCJ, has said, 'Still from far too many pulpits the old stereotypes are thoughtlessly re-cycled. The task of educating the Christian clergy has to be done afresh in every generation.' Still, too often, the story of Jesus' Passion and Crucifixion is read in church without any explanation that it was the Roman authorities that crucified Jesus and that, even if some Jewish leaders wanted Jesus 'out of the way,' other Jews were his followers and supporters.

Tackling Extremism

CCJ's commitment to religious tolerance and its opposition to all forms of discrimination continues to be its priority.

In tackling the dangers of extremism and the misuse of religion to sanction violence, CCJ's long years of work with local communities means that it has had valuable and in many ways unique experience to share in the new situation. This, in turn, has brought a renewed awareness of the importance of CCJ and the contribution it can make to 'Community Cohesion,' which became part of the Labour government's agenda under Tony Blair.

To meet this new situation, since 2006, CCJ's work has been focussed on specific projects. Five projects were identified at that time: Root and Branch; *Yehi Or* (Let there be Light); Shoulder to Shoulder; Citizenship, Identity and Difference (CID); and *Tête-à-tête*. Other programmes have subsequently been added including Yad Vashem seminars, City Business seminars, Encounters, and Micro Image.

Root and Branch

The objectives of 'Root and Branch' were to train branches in community dialogue, to strengthen relations between different faith communities and to improve internal and external communications. In pursuing this in 2006, a new format newsletter 'Dialogue' was introduced. Staff visited branches to listen to them and to encourage them. The Branch Consultative Group was formed and met regularly.

In 2008 another project called 'Lives and Voices' developed from Root and Branch. This involved several schools in the London Basin and Kent and encouraged Jewish, Afro-Caribbean, and Muslim students as well as Hindu and Sikh students from Asia or East Africa to look at and compare the stories of their parents' or grandparents' arrival in Britain.

In 2008 CCJ partnered the Board of Deputies in its 'Shared Futures' programme. CCJ also helped a community college in South London to establish a multi-faith chaplaincy

Yehi Or

The objectives of the second project *Yehi Or*, 'Let there be Light.' were to create informed networks in faith communities to combat antisemitism and religious intolerance as well as addressing anti-Judaism and to enabling more effective dialogue between Jews and Christians.

Two seminars in the new Tony Prendergast Seminar Series

were held at Sarum College, Salisbury. They were designed to make Christian lay ministers more aware of anti-Judaism in Christian liturgy and teaching. The annual summer school at Ammerdown, which in 2006 was on 'Abraham,' became part of this project. Two seminars on 'Repentance and Forgiveness' were also held. Response to day-to-day events, issuing press statements and writing articles also became part of this project.

In 2008, further successful 'Tony Prendergast' seminars were held, one in the Newcastle diocese and one in London. As well as the CCJ summer school, a pilot workshop on Judaism and Jewish Christian dialogue was held at Ripon Theological College, Cuddesdon, near Oxford. This was so worthwhile that it has been repeated every year since.

In the following year an excellent day for lay Christian leaders looking at Rites of Passage was held at a synagogue in London. This included the chance to observe a Bar Mitzvah as guests of the family.

Shoulder to Shoulder

'Shoulder to Shoulder' was the third project aimed to promote a balanced understanding of the Middle East crisis among Christian leaders and opinion-formers. A number of briefings were held at different locations. The annual study tour to Israel and the Palestinian territories, once again led by Mrs Beryl Norman, became part of this project. Further briefings arranged in partnership with the Anglo-Israel Association were held in 2008.

Citizenship, Identity and Difference'

The fourth project was called 'Citizenship, Identity and Difference'(CID). This was intended to promote understanding of interfaith issues in schools by providing helpful educational material for teachers. Initially this involved extensive consultation with teachers and educational advisors. In 2008 much effort was put into producing a DVD, in partnership with the Aegis Trust. Students from different faiths were used as the actors.

Tête-à-tête: Side by Side

'Tête-à-tête' or 'Side by Side' as this programme was subsequently renamed - focussed on encouraging interfaith activities at universities and reducing tensions on UK campuses. In this work, CCJ established close co-operation with other bodies such as the Student Christian Movement, the Three Faiths Forum and the Agency for Jewish Sixth Formers. Another Youth Study Tour to Israel/Palestine was arranged and also a special dinner for young people at Salters' Hall, in the City of London, to mark the 350th anniversary of the resettlement of Jews in Britain.

In 2007 it was decided to concentrate on offering practical help to chaplains of all faiths in colleges of Higher and Further Education. Pilot workshops on 'Extremism on Campus' were held in Guildford, London and Newcastle.

Successful seminars were held on Jewish, Christian and Muslim Relations, at Sarum College, and on the Holocaust at the Yad Vashem Institute in Jerusalem. An electronic magazine or 'e-zine' was developed by Michael Wakelin, specifically to help chaplains with interfaith issues on Higher Education campuses.

Encounters

'Encounters' is a related programme under which seminars on Jewish-Christian relations have been arranged at a number of theological colleges and have included visits to the Beth Shalom Holocaust Centre at Laxton in Nottinghamshire. In 2011 fifty students participated in the programme.

Another aspect of this programme has been the very valuable twice yearly conversations between rabbis from across the Jewish community with Black Pentecostal pastors. The project is arranged in co-operation with Churches Together in Britain and Ireland (CTBI) and the Board of Deputies of British Jews. The conversaziones have explored experiences of exile, slavery and ostracism as well as the strength of communal solidarity.

Besides this pro-active work, a lot of time is taken up - in CCJ's Chief Executive David Gifford's words - in 'putting out fires.' Many of these occasions will be discussed in later chapters, but questions about admissions policies for faith schools belong here.

Admissions Policies for Faith Schools

The issue was highlighted by a decision of JFS (formerly the Jewish Free School) not to admit a boy because his standing as a Jew was questionable because his mother's conversion was under the auspices of a non-Orthodox synagogue. The School denied a place to a child, because it did not recognise the mother's conversion and therefore did not regard the child as Jewish. In June 2009, the Court of

Appeal ruled that the school had acted unlawfully. In the Court's view, the school's selection criteria were based on ethnicity, which amounted to discrimination on racial grounds. The Court accepted that discrimination on the basis of religious observance was permissible but not on matrilineal descent.

The Board of Deputies of British Jews has argued that although the definition of a Jew is a matter of much debate in the Jewish community, it is up to the Jewish community itself and the not civil courts to decide on this issue. It also objected to applying an observance test as it may encourage Jewish families to feign religious observance or may mean that some Jewish parents, who may not be very observant, will be denied the opportunity to give their children a Jewish education. Eventually the Supreme Court ruled against the school. More recently, the basis on which children are admitted to Church of England schools has become a matter of debate.

Islam and Islamaphobia

There was also discussion of a draft Position Statement on 'Islam and Islamaphobia. It was hoped that CCJ's experience in building good relations between Jews and Christians might be of value more widely. There was also further discussion about the role of the Advisory Board, which had suffered from lack of direction and purpose for a number of years. The Chairman Bishop Nigel McCulloch and the Chief Executive Officer were anxious that this Constitutional body might be resurrected and contribute once again to the work of CCJ.

2009 saw several new projects emerge as part of CCJ's portfolio. An important unique and exciting initiative was arranging City Business Breakfast seminars, which are described in more detail in the chapter 'Facing the Future.'

Publications

Besides many talks and meetings, CCJ has through the years used every available means to communicate its message.

Common Ground

The importance of *Common Ground* as an educational tool cannot be over-estimated.

Dr Harry Levy, for so many years its editor, looking back over his collection of copies dating back to 1949, wrote, 'I feel moved to wonder whether the wider community is aware of the debt it owes to CCJ for promoting such a journal... As a mouthpiece for the furtherance of healthy relations between Jews and Christians *Common Ground* occupies a unique place in the religious press.'

At the beginning of the nineties the format of *Common Ground* was dramatically changed. Instead of an A 5 black and white text, it was transformed into an A4 glossy publication with colour and pictures. This was thanks, in large measure, to the energy, enthusiasm and generosity of Elizabeth Maxwell and professional designers. The first issue of the new *Common Ground* was warmly welcomed. 'I find the new format most impressive and educational,' wrote Harry Levy. Dr Bernard Resnikoff, of the American Jewish Committee in Israel, wrote, 'I found the entire issue creative, original and most exciting ... Please accept my congratulations for a first-rate job.' More recently, *Common Ground* was presented with an award by the Board of Deputies.

During the last twenty years the range and quality of the articles as well as the attractive format has enhanced the prestige of CCJ. Such a high quality publication, of course, needs the time of members of staff and of volunteers, and also needs to be paid for. In 2008 a reassessment was made of the best and most cost-effective distribution of the CCJ's journal *Common Ground*. Only 8,000 copies of *Common Ground* were to be printed – down from 20,000. It was, however, to be available to clergy in PDF format. That year only one issue was published. More recently a foundation, recognising the major contribution the journal has made to Jewish-Christian understanding, has sponsored *Common Ground*.

For some years *Common Ground* included a beautifully produced coloured educational supplement 'Learning Together,' which was a valuable resource for RE teachers to collect. Subjects covered included 'Celebrating Harvest,' 'Purim and Epiphany' and 'Church and Synagogue.'

Since 2007 issues of *Common Ground* have had a particular focus. This makes the journal something to be collected and kept for future reference. In April 2007, to coincide with events marking the abolition of slavery in the British Empire, the theme was "Survivor," with moving stories of heroism and fortitude in the face of persecution and prejudice. The 2009 Spring issue concentrated on the Psalms with a variety of contributors sharing what a particular psalm meant to them. The 2009 Winter issue concentrated on Antisemitism, which was particularly important at a time when the number of antisemitic attacks was increasing. The 2010 Summer issue provided a wide variety of articles to give Christians a better understanding of Judaism. Many of the articles in the 2010 Winter issue relate in varying ways to Jerusalem - for example, its archaeology as well as Blake's poem 'Jerusalem.' The Summer 2011 issue on Israel was well received. The 2011 Winter *Common Ground* was a special edition to mark the 70th Anniversary of the CCJ, with articles that look back and that look forward.

Booklets

CCJ's publications have also been very important educational tools. The long running 'Education Series,' included the following titles: 'Who are the Jews? What is their faith?'; 'Shabbat – the Jewish Sabbath;' 'The Christian Sunday;' 'The Synagogue;' 'The Jewish home;' and 'Who are the Christians? What is their faith?'

In addition CCJ published a 'Study Series,' including 'CCJ and Israel;' 'Jews and Christians: What do the Churches Say;' 'Christian-Jewish Relations: A new look;' 'Teaching the Holocaust – Dilemmas and Responses;' 'The Holocaust – its relevance to every Christian;' and 'Hard Sayings – Difficult New Testament Texts for Jewish-Christian Dialogue.'

When it was decided to have a national day of Remembrance of the Holocaust, CCJ produced excellent resources for teachers. *The Holocaust: Faith, Morality and Ethics*, edited by Jane Clements, Jonathan Gorsky and Rosie Boston, is especially valuable.

Members of staff have also contributed to 'Words for Today' - published by the International Bible Reading Fellowship - which is widely read by Christians.

From Filmstrips to DVDs

Technology changes, but the message remains the same. Filmstrips for schools became slide/tape shows. Then in 1998 CCJ produced a video 'Judaism Lives,' together with back-up notes. More recently the CID (Citizenship, Identity and Difference) project produced a DVD that was also uploaded onto the internet for wider distribution.

Exhibitions

CCJ also acts as a bulletin board to publicise relevant exhibitions, such as the Anne Frank Exhibition or the Board of Deputies' 'Living Judaism.' CCJ also collaborates with a wide range of other educational bodies, such as the Shapiro Institute, the Jewish Musical Festival, the London Jewish Cultural Centre and the Jewish Book Week.

Media

Reports of CCJ activities are regularly featured in the religious press and in local newspapers. The national and religious press quote from CCJ Press Statements and letters on controversial issues are often published. CCJ also has an informative website that is reviewed regularly and in 2011 a completely new website was launched.

On many occasions staff members have been interviewed or asked to speak on the radio and have taken part in broadcast religious programmes.

The contribution of CCJ's educational work to ensuring that Britain remains a tolerant and harmonious society cannot be over-estimated. It is important for young people to recognise the benefits of growing up in an increasingly multi-cultural and multi-faith society and world. They need also to be aware of the dangers of intolerance and racism and xenophobia. Yet it should never be forgotten that knowledge of each other's religious beliefs and practices is enriching for Jews and Christians in its own right. As David Gifford has said, 'CCJ is active in promoting information and knowledge exchange *for its own sake* as well as part of the fight against antisemitism and xenophobia in times of economic challenge and social and political change.'

Chapter 4. The Continuing struggle against Antisemitism

'Antisemitism: A Very Light Sleeper'
Runnymede Trust publication 1994

Antisemitism

Member of Parliament Denis MacShane, in his recent book *Globalising Hatred: the New Antisemitism,* makes clear 'that anti-Semitism has many different facets. It is both an expression of racism and yet also has deep religious roots. It is social, and appeals to intellectuals who look for networks and secret influences to explain state politics... It is the world's most pernicious ideology and practice, international in its reach and capable of taking different forms from the university campus to the upper-class dinner party.'

'To work for the elimination of religious and racial prejudice, hatred and discrimination, 'particularly anti-Semitism,' 'is one of the aims that its founders set for the Council of Christians and Jews in 1942. Seventy years later, 'elimination' seems an over-optimistic word. Antisemitism is indeed like the many-headed monster Hydra, of Greek mythology, who sprouted two heads for every head that was cut off. A trawl through some websites, which I do not recommend, shows just how virulent and pernicious antisemitism still is today.

'Antisemitism' was the word used by Wilhelm Marr (1819-1904), who founded the League of Anti-Semites. It was a racist doctrine based on the false assumption that, just as languages are differentiated as having 'Aryan' or 'Semitic' roots, so there are corresponding racial groups of which the Aryan one is superior. This quasi-scientific misuse of the theory of evolution expressed itself not only in antisemitism, but also in apartheid and some nineteenth century imperialist attitudes. Marr deliberately chose the word 'antisemitism' rather than the existing term *Judenhass* (Jew-hatred), which had religious overtones.

If the word antisemitism only dates back to the nineteenth century, its reality goes back to the Ancient World. Centuries of anti-Jewish teaching by the Churches exacerbated this latent prejudice. Most Churches now recognise this and admit that their anti-Jewish teaching 'provided the soil in which the evil weed of Nazism was able to take root and spread its poison.' At the Kristallnacht Memorial meeting in 1988, Archbishop Robert Runcie took the lead in confessing the Churches' shameful record:

> 'Without centuries of Christian anti-Semitism, Hitler's passionate hatred would never have been so fervently echoed ... The tragedy of Kristallnacht and all that followed is that so much was perpetrated in Christ's name. To glorify the Third Reich, the Christian faith was betrayed ... And even today there are many Christians who fail to see this as self-evident. And why this blindness? Because for centuries Christians have held Jews collectively responsible for the death of Jesus. On Good Friday Jews have, in time past, cowered behind locked doors for fear of a Christian mob seeking 'revenge' for deicide. Without the poisoning of Christian minds through the centuries, the Holocaust is unthinkable.'

CCJ has been a prime mover in persuading Christians to recognise that the traditional teaching of the Churches that God had punished the Jews for killing their Messiah by exiling them from the Land of Promise is historically, theologically and morally wrong and a cause of great suffering to the Jewish people. Much more still needs to be done to ensure that congregations are more aware of these far-reaching changes and do not perpetuate past prejudice by their choice of hymns and readings.

Symbolic Acts

Symbolic acts are a powerful way to expressing penitence and the desire for a new relationship. In 1990 the 800th anniversary of the tragic outbreak of anti-Jewish violence in York was remembered at Clifford's Tower. It was there that, besieged by the barons and an angry mob, some '150 Jews and Jewesses chose to die at each other's hands rather than renounce their faith'. There was a memorial gathering at the tower conducted by the then Archbishop of York, Dr John Habgood and Rabbi Dr Norman Solomon. There were also special services at the Synagogue and the Cathedral, as well as a concert and a conference.

In January 2001, the city of Leicester condemned the antisemitism of its foundation. Simon de Montfort's charter of about 1231 stated that 'No Jew or Jewess in my time, or in the time of any of my heirs to the end of the world, shall inhabit or remain, or obtain residence in the city of Leicester.' Jews have in fact been living in Leicester since the early 1840s and some people criticised the Council's action as 'political correctness run wild.' The leader of the Council, Councillor Ross Willmot, said that renouncing the

Charter re-emphasised Leicester's high tolerance of all cultures, particularly in advance of the National Holocaust Memorial Day. The hate mail received by the Council only went to demonstrate the importance of the action. 'There is still antisemitism here.' Councillor Willmot, who is from a Jewish background, also said that the event was very personal for him. 'I would not be allowed to be leader of the Council because I would not be allowed to be in this city.'

The Churches' Condemnation of antisemitism

The Churches, in many official statements, have rejected past anti-Judaism. Modern antisemitism, therefore, as the Runnymede Report said, tends to be quasi-racial, in that it is Jews as a people who are the objects of prejudice, rather than the religion.'

This means that Christian leaders, as did those who founded CCJ, now stand shoulder to shoulder in opposition to antisemitism. In 2004, on Holocaust Memorial Day, *The Times* published a letter from the Joint-Presidents of CCJ, who wrote that 'As Presidents of CCJ, we agree that antisemitism is abhorrent. It is an attempt to dehumanise a part of humanity by making it a scapegoat for shared ills. We pledge ourselves once more to combat all forms of racism, prejudice and xenophobia.'

In a statement to mark Holocaust Memorial Day in 2006 Archbishop Rowan Williams called on faith communities to demonstrate their abhorrence of antisemitism and ensure 'that it finds not the smallest foothold in our churches, mosques, gurdwaras or temples.' The Archbishop added, 'Is it not a matter of the gravest concern that a religious community in this country must, on the advice of the police, put in place a range of security measures for its worship, the education of its children and its social activities? For what other religious community is this systematically the case? This is serious enough, but elsewhere there are inflammatory, bigoted and irresponsible statements made even by some in prominent public positions.'

Holocaust denial

One form antisemitism takes is Holocaust Denial. In its crudest expression it claims that the concentration camps and the murder of six million Jews was a 'myth' designed to gain sympathy for the Jews and their hopes of establishing the State of Israel. A more subtle form of Holocaust denial is the attempt - sometimes called 'Revisionism' - to re-write history and exonerate Hitler or see Nazism as a response to the 'unfair' Treaty of Versailles at the end of World War I.

Perhaps the most insidious form of Holocaust denial is to see the Shoah as just one more of 'the terrible things that happen in war' and to ignore the very specific nature of the cold-blooded attempt to exterminate all Jews. The 'Hitler Museum' website, for example, says 'The museum, while acknowledging the tragedy that over 50 million people died during World War II, retains its non-biased status by refraining from making political judgments of any sort.' There is a similar claim to being unbiased on the Hitler's Speeches website, which says 'Even the ideological enemies of Adolf Hitler will admit that he was a highly gifted and prolific speaker.'

The dangers of Holocaust denial make it essential that the Holocaust is not forgotten. 'Education about the Shoah is a central concern of the Council of Christians and Jews, which seeks an in-depth understanding of its impact on Jews, Christians and the relationship between them,' wrote Sister Margaret Shepherd in her moving account of CCJ's special visit to Poland in 1999. 'In the space of five days we visited Majdanek; the labour camp at Plaszow and Schindler's factory; Auschwitz-Birkenau; the Warsaw Ghetto and Treblinka.'

CCJ has also produced *The Holocaust: Faith, Morality and Ethics*, which is an excellent resource for teachers.

Holocaust Museums

Besides its own direct contribution to Holocaust education, CCJ has also actively supported plans for the Holocaust Exhibition at the Imperial War Museum and the establishment of a Holocaust Memorial Day.

Suzanne Bardgett, Project Director of the Imperial War Museum Holocaust exhibition, wrote in 1997 – three years before the Exhibition opened – of the enormous amount of material that had to be examined. It was agreed by the exhibition designers that photographs are the most powerful and immediate kind of testimony – especially if they tell the story of a family or individual. Each of the six million people who were murdered was a unique individual with his or her own story. 'Amateur snapshots taken by witnesses to killings, recorded with unknowable thoughts or judgement gives the scene a chilling freshness.'

The Museum's Holocaust Exhibition takes as its starting point the turbulent political scene in Europe immediately after the First World War. The exhibition then traces the rise of the Nazi party; how antisemitism as a Europe-wide phenomenon made a fertile seedbed for Hitler's anti-Jewish beliefs; the perversion of science to support Nazi race theory; the isolation of German Jews, the refugee crisis and the advent of so-called 'Euthanasia' policies in 1939.

Photographs, documents, newspapers, artefacts, posters and film offer stark evidence of persecution and slaughter, collaboration and resistance. A funeral cart from the Warsaw Ghetto sits adjacent to diaries and photograph albums of those who died through hunger and disease. Part of a deportation railcar - given by Belgian Railways - is on display and visitors can walk up onto a wagon, which was once heaved by slave labourers in a concentration camp.

Contrasting with the story of industrialised murder is that of the men, women and children who endured Nazi policies and in most cases died as a result of them.

Toys, diaries, photograph albums, story books, hand-made mementos - these remnants show individual efforts at survival, while the testimony of eighteen survivors of the Holocaust brings a fresh and haunting perspective to the narrative; how families responded to the direst circumstances; the resilience and luck which allowed some to survive.

Five years before the opening of the Holocaust Museum, the Beth Shalom Holocaust Centre at Laxton in

Nottinghamshire had been established. The Centre is the personal initiative of Stephen D Smith and his brother James, who were deeply moved by their visits to Israel and Birkenau. 'Beth Shalom, the House of Peace, is not a monument but a memorial to the victims of the Shoah and a center of learning for future generations.' Stephen Smith insists that 'the Shoah was not about the suffering of the Jews, but about the suffering of humanity as experienced by the Jews of Europe. 'This is why it is concerned with racism and genocide as well as anti-Semitism. The Centre says to the Jewish community that somewhat belatedly some Christians are beginning to realize that the Shoah is their problem too and are prepared to do something practical about its meaning.'

The Holocaust Centre, visited by many school parties as well as adults, promotes an understanding of the roots of discrimination and prejudice, and the development of ethical values, leading to a greater understanding within society. The Centre uses the history of genocide as a model of how society can break down. It also emphasises how current and future generations must carefully examine and learn from these tragedies. The Centre promotes respect for human rights, equal opportunities and good citizenship, which has greater resonance than ever in our culturally diverse society.

The Holocaust Centre offers opportunities for people of all backgrounds to explore the history and implications of these tragic events. These include the Holocaust exhibition, memorial gardens, and a bookshop. There are also seminar and research facilities for students, teachers, scholars, professionals and many others.

Holocaust Memorial Day

CCJ was one of the bodies consulted about proposals for a Holocaust Memorial Day. CCJ said that the emphasis should be on the future and our common humanity. 'The post-war history of Jewish-Christian reconciliation should inspire a similar search for peace and understanding in areas of the world where people have suffered at the hands of their neighbours. ... The day should therefore focus on the universal lessons of the Holocaust and be inclusive.' It was also said that 'the day should highlight rescue, resistance and inspiring responses.' It was suggested that emphasis should be given to encouraging schools to teach about the Holocaust. Suggested themes were: Persecution of minorities, Solidarity, Asylum, Forgiveness and Reconciliation, Rescuers as well as Lessons for Today. Certainly these themes had a universal relevance, but one may wonder whether the uniqueness of the Shoah was being evaded.

The subsequent issue of *Common Ground*, however, included an article arguing against Holocaust Memorial Day by the Methodist leader Leslie Griffiths, who had been chair of Golders Green and Hendon CCJ. After seeing 'Schindler's List,' he was worried that over familiarity might acclimatise people to such evil.

Leslie Griffiths' cautionary note is a reminder that, while Christians should remember the Holocaust, they need to be sensitive in how they do this especially if they arrange a Christian service to mark Holocaust Memorial Day. It is important to avoid imposing a Christian meaning on the murder of so many Jews. A number of CCJ branches arrange special acts of commemoration on Holocaust Memorial Day or on Yom Ha Shoah, which is the day chosen by the state of Israel for the remembrance of those who were murdered.

Remembering for the Future

Remembering the Holocaust is not just about the past. It is vital to ensure that such an atrocity is never repeated. After a joint visit to Auschwitz-Birkenau with the Chief Rabbi Lord Sacks, Archbishop Rowan Williams said it is not enough to say that '"the evil was past understanding," because if we do, how shall we be able to read the signs of the times, the indications that evil is gathering force once again and societies are slipping towards the same collective corruption and moral sickness that made the Shoah possible... Distorted religion, fear of the stranger, the reduction of humans to functions and numbers, the obsession with technological solutions that take no account of human particularity – Auschwitz is more than the sum of the parts, but it would not have happened without them. They are still at work in our world.' The Chief Rabbi, likewise, insisted that 'by remembering the past, we can change the future. Hate has not vanished from our world, nor have war, violence and terror. That is why we must still remember.' He also said, 'the fact that we can come together, people of all faiths, to experience an environment where one faith was persecuted - isn't that a measure of how far we have come.'

Antisemitism has many disguises.

Nazi pseudo-scientific racism which led to the Shoah is, of course, the most terrible expression of antisemitism, but, as noted at the beginning of this chapter, antisemitism is present under many disguises. Some examples are the language used in criticism of Israeli actions. Animal rights campaigners who protest about *Shechita* may be infiltrated by neo-Nazis and those who express disquiet about male circumcision may find they have antisemitic supporters.

In 2002 Mr Mike Whine from the Board of Deputies spoke about growing antisemitism in Europe. The past decade has, also, seen a worrying increase in antisemitic incidents in Britain.

Antisemitism often masquerades as anti-Zionism. Criticism of the policies of Israeli governments may be acceptable, but such criticism easily turns into a denial of Israel's right to exist and even of Jews right to life. Soon after the Gaza campaign – two hundred and twenty anti-Semitic incidents were recorded by the police. 'Jewish buildings are daubed with anti-Semitic graffiti. Jews are attacked in the street. ... Anti-Israel demonstrators shout' "Kill the Jews", "Be afraid, Jews," "Heil Hitler," and "Jews to the gas". Worshippers on their way to the synagogue at which I pray,' said the Chief Rabbi, 'are shouted at by a passer-by with the words, "Hitler should have finished the job."' By contrast criticism, for example, of the actions of the USA in Iraq does not become a call to kill all Americans.

At other times, antisemites have infiltrated the Animal Rights movement. Genuine concern about animal rights may lead some to argue that Shechita – the Jewish way of slaughtering animals - and *Halal* - the Muslim method - are cruel. Defenders say that these are the most humane way to kill animals: many Gentiles disagree. This is not the place to discuss the rights and wrongs of *Shechita*. The danger is that questioning *Shechita* is used by antisemites to attack Jews *per se*.

Chas Newkey-Burden, on Totally Jewish.com, has said,
'I wonder how many of those involved in the anti-shechita campaign genuinely care about animals. Have they not listened to the experts who declare shechita is the most humane form of slaughter? The campaigners' motivations are often suspect.' As Shechita UK said: "There are also those whose opposition has little to do with animal welfare, but is motivated by ill-will toward Jews." This is a serious accusation and one that is made with justification. I am reminded of those who protest so noisily against Israel. Their protestations would appear more sincere if they even occasionally acknowledged that there are conflicts and controversies elsewhere in the world.'

In the same way those in the wider community who express disquiet about male circumcision - and this is often an issue when a Jew marries a Christian - may find antisemites among their allies. Sometimes the arguments for and against are on medical issues, but there is also the question whether the state should legislate to ban practices which are required by a particular faith tradition.

There is also a danger that extreme Muslims repeat antisemitic lies in their anger at Israeli policies, despite the condemnation of such views by Muslim leaders. There are persistent reports that copies of the notorious anti-Jewish forgery *The Protocols of Zion* are on sale at some mosques.

Bishop Nigel McCulloch, Chair of CCJ, has also warned that government cuts and growing unemployment may increase religious intolerance. Various opinion polls show that many Europeans think that Jews have too much power in business. Hostility to Muslims is also increasing.

Those who in the darkest days of World War II met together to found CCJ were right to see that the attempt to eliminate antisemitism is inextricably linked to the elimination of religious and racial prejudice, hatred and discrimination. The problem is that few perpetrators of prejudice are likely to have much contact with CCJ or to be willing to listen to reason. Many are hostile to any form of religion. The responsible leaders, however, of all faith communities in Britain, working together through the Inter Faith Network for the UK, of which CCJ is an active member, are united in working for tolerance and understanding and in promoting the ethical values that they share. Congregations need to make this a higher priority.

Chapter 5   The State of Israel: Cause of Misunderstanding

'The issue of Israel is too sensitive and too crucial to be ignored.' Sir Michael Latham

The long running dispute between Israel and the Palestinian Territories, or Israel/Palestine as many people now refer to it, has been the most problematic of all issues with which CCJ has had to deal. There is, however, a limit to what CCJ can do. CCJ is a British charity, but most British Jews have a close bond with Jews who live in Israel. The creation of the State of Israel has had a profound effect on all Jews whether or not they live there. It has been described as a 'shift of paradigms – from diasporic homelessness to landed return and from hapless victimhood to control over our own destiny…The fact is that we British Jews have been changed (whether we like it or not) by the establishment of the State of Israel.' Consequently, events in the Middle East have a significant impact on Christian-Jewish relations in the UK. They also have an impact on the relations of both communities with the Muslim community and the secular world. As a charity, CCJ is not allowed to be involved in political campaigning, but anti-Israel protests are often a cloak for antisemitism and in some quarters, wrongly, Zionism is seen as a form of racism.

Christian members of CCJ affirm Israel's legitimate place among the nations of the world. Archbishop Rowan Williams in a Rosh Hashanah message in 2010 once again affirmed that 'the State of Israel is a legitimate, democratic and law governed state that exists by consent of the United Nations and has its place in the councils of states in the world. In the light of twentieth century history, it is crucial that there is a state in the world where it is unequivocally safe to be Jewish.' The Archbishop, in his Rosh Hashanah message, also voiced CCJ's hope that 'Jews, Christians and Muslims would be able to pray together for peace and justice' and refrain 'from words and actions which are partisan rather than reconciling.'

Christians, however, also have bonds with fellow believers in the area. Most of them are Palestinians, but there are also some Messianic Jews. Christian charities are also active in the West Bank. They sense the suffering of the local population and feel called to be 'a voice for the voiceless.' Some relief organisations such as 'Christian Aid' have been critical of Israel's human rights record. CCJ has recognised this and *Common Ground* has published articles about various charities such as 'Action around Bethlehem for Children with Disability.' (ABCD).

The recent historical and political background.

At the start of the nineties, the first Intifada was under way, but then in August 1993 the secretly agreed *Oslo Accord* was made public. A month later, Prime Minister Rabin's uneasy handshake with Arafat was watched on television by millions of people around the world. Agreement was signed in Cairo on May 4th, 1994. A further agreement, Oslo II, was signed in September 1994, but progress was abruptly halted by the assassination of Yitzak Rabin and by the election in 1996 of Benjamin Netanyahu as Prime Minister.

Yet, when Ehud Barak became Prime Minister in 1999 hopes for peace were revived and running high at the start of the new decade when Pope John Paul II made his historic visit to the Holy Land.

These hopes were soon dashed, when, despite President Bill Clinton's best efforts, Prime Minister Barak and President Arafat failed to reach agreement at Camp David. The first decade of this century has been a troubled time, internationally and in Israel.

There is no need to record all the conflict that has followed the 9/11 attack on the World Trade Towers. There were many less well-known positive responses. One of these was a journey, soon afterwards to Israel, of CCJ's Director and Associate Director, Sr Margaret Shepherd and Jane Clements. They were encouraged by the recognition there of the importance of CCJ's work. 'You are at the cutting edge,' said Gadi Golan, Head of Interreligious Affairs at Israel's Foreign Office. Another official said to Sister Margaret, 'Oh, what beautiful work you do.'

Renewed violence marked the start of the Second Intifada. In response to the deadly attacks of suicide bombers, Israel increased security at check points and embarked on building the *Security Barrier* – both measures of which made life much more difficult for many Palestinians living in the West Bank. The Israeli withdrawal from Gaza failed to achieve the disengagement that was hoped for. Hamas, an avowedly Islamist party, which does not recognise Israel's right to exist, gained power in Gaza. Shelling of Israeli towns from Gaza continued and this was met by punitive measures and then at the end of December 2008 by a full scale conflict, which caused many civilian deaths. Talk of peace negotiations continues, but, writing in 2012, little progress has been made.

The challenge of the right response

CCJ's main work in this field, as in others, is informational. The terms of reference for the Israel Advisory Committee, which was re-established in June 1990, gives a good summary of CCJ's role *vis-a-vis* Israel. Its brief was to study the situation; to educate and inform Christians about Israel; to monitor the media - especially the religious press; to produce briefing materials; to encourage dialogue about Israel and to explore theologically the concepts of Land and Covenant. It was agreed that there might be informal contact with Muslims.

As might be expected this Advisory Committee was very active. In 1993, for example, a meeting for clergy in South London was arranged; a lunch for the religious press correspondents was addressed by Mr Daniel Rossing of the Melitz Centre for Encounter in Israel; and a Church Leaders Tour was organised.

Study Tours to Israel

Study tours to Israel have been an important aspect of CCJ's educational work. During the last twenty years – thanks to successful fund-raising - CCJ has arranged tours to Israel-Palestine for its members, for Young Adults and for Church leaders.

The Church Leaders tours have had a lasting impact on most of the participants. Professor Ursula King of Bristol

University wrote of the 1993 tour that it 'was a journey of discovery and something of an existential pilgrimage.' 'Never before,' she said of the visit to Yad Vashem, 'have I experienced the powers of death and darkness with such force.' Margaret Staple, who took part in the Church Leaders tour in April 1991, wrote of it as a time 'of heightened experience and enhanced awareness' and a 'larger-than-life episode.' She entitled her article 'Confronting Realities.' Richard Harries, described the 1995 tour, as 'an amazing and valuable experience.'

'All CCJ tours of Israel are exceptional' wrote Beryl Norman, who has led many of them. 'They offer a deep experience of Israel, past and present and of its many people of whom we meet a wide cross section.' The tours enable first hand encounter with Judaism and Christianity in the Land and offer a chance to explore the Land itself – cities, lakes, hills and deserts. Most of the tours are arranged in conjunction with the Melitz Centre for Encounter. Some of the tours have a special focus. In the 1997 tour, participants set out to discover how Judaism and Christianity drew apart.' The 2001 tour had an archaeological emphasis, including visits to Lakhish, Be'er Sheva, Meggido, Tsippori, Bet Saida, and Dan. The group also spent Shabbat at the religious Kibbutz Lavi and on Sunday morning were invited to a local Greek Catholic church.'

For many Young Adults the tours are an unforgettable experience. 'Israel has had a profound effect upon my life, both personally and academically,' said Andrew Rogers. Sophie Capitanchik, on the 1996 Young Adult's Tour, was in Tel Aviv soon after a devastating suicide bomber attack. 'Yet throughout the unrest of generations, the tiny country of

Israel deals with its own pain, and remembering, moves on. This journey was an opportunity to try to understand how this is possible, for the people and the land ... I feel for Israel, for its people, for the land and for God's plan for it.' Catherine Brewer said of the tour in the year 2000 that it made her face 'the question of how to affirm one's own identity without negating, diminishing or excluding others.' The theme of the 2005 Young Adults Tour was 'Yes to Reconciliation' – meeting with and listening to those who seek peace. Debbie Young, who was CCJ Youth Officer in 2003-2004, was particularly concerned to support peace efforts in Israel/Palestine.

In 2004 instead of a tour to Israel, CCJ arranged a Holy Land Dialogue Conference in London with the participation of the leaders of Haviva, Merchavim and the organizers of Melitz Tours. Bethlehem International Centre's Media Co-ordinator was not able to gain permission to travel.

Yad Vashem

In 2009 a new initiative was to arrange a ten-day seminar on the Holocaust at Yad Vashem. As part of its educational work CCJ has produced some booklets. Almost every issue of *Common Ground* has several articles, which relate to Israel. Many of these help to make known groups in Israel and Palestine – usually ignored by the media - who are working for justice, reconciliation and peace. The 2007 autumn edition of *Common Ground,* which focussed on Israel was well received. Staff members continually give talks on the situation and also write articles and comment in the press.

Support for Interfaith Groups in Israel

CCJ has helped to publicise some of the many organisations in Israel that are working for peace and inter-religious cooperation.

Neve Shalom/Wahat-al-Salam, which is a community, founded by Fr Bruno Hussar in 1972, where Jewish, Muslim and Christian Israeli families live together, was the subject of a full-length article in *Common Ground* in 1993. The School for Peace there runs a variety of courses on conflict resolution.

'Open House's' co-director Yehezkel Landau wrote in *Common Ground* in 1998 (Israel's 50th Anniversary Year.) 'The Open House Centre was founded in 1991 to further peace and coexistence among Israeli Arabs and Jews in the mixed city of Ramle. It has two inter-related goals: to provide educational and social opportunities to Arab children and their families through its Centre for the Development of the Arab Child; and to be a place of encounter and cooperation between Jews and Arabs in the Ramle-Lod area through its Centre for Jewish-Arab Coexistence. In his article, Yehezkel Landau deplored lack of vision among the leaders but insisted that 'small miracles of transformed individuals can generate large miracles on the scale we have witnessed in the former Communist bloc.'

CCJ has also supported 'Common Future', 'Merchavim' and Givat Haviva. 'Common Future' is a project in Galilee inspired by Neil Harris. 'Merchavim' is led by Mike Prashnser. Both he and his colleagues and Neil Harris visited the CCJ offices in 2002. In 2003, Mike Flax of Givat Haviva, which is the national centre of Kibbutz Arti, a major kibbutz movement, came to the office. The centre has Jewish and Arab educators seeking to break down prejudice. Tragically soon after the visit, two teenagers who were taking part in one the Centre's programmes were killed in the Haifa bus bombing.

Rabbis for Peace sent a letter to *Common Ground*, which was published in 1997 'Two questions may be circulating in your mind,' the letter says. 'How can we maintain any kind of partnership with Palestinian leadership and individuals during these frightening times, when Jewish children shopping for notebooks do not survive a chance encounter with an Islamic suicide bomber on the Ben Yehudah Mall? And even if we can justify dialogue strategically and intellectually, where do we find the emotional and spiritual energy to work for the human rights of those who are our enemies? We continue to believe that the reduction, if not elimination, of violations of human rights requires a political solution to our conflict and that unilaterally withdrawing from the Oslo process is not an option, because it would not only reward terror, but further fuel it. Our work is based on the fundamental inclusive principle that there is a divine spark in all human beings, and trampling on human dignity is a blasphemous act.'

The same issue had an article about Revd Petra Helt who, as Secretary of the Ecumenical Theological Research Fraternity in Israel, was deeply committed to dialogue. Despite being seriously wounded in the terrorist bomb blast in Mahaneh Yehuda market, she remained firm in her belief that every person intrinsically deserves respect.

CCJ also has close links with the Interreligious Co-ordinating Council in Israel, led with great dedication for many years by Dr Ron Kronish and the Interfaith Encounter Association (IEA), led by Yehuda Stovlov. There are many other groups that CCJ supports, including the Jerusalem Women's Interfaith Group and the Parents Circle Family Forum, for parents whose children have been killed in the conflict.

Good News

Despite so much depressing news from the Middle East, there has been encouraging progress in both Roman Catholic (discussed in a later chapter) and Anglican relations with Israel – despite Synod debates!

In January 2002 Archbishop George Carey, who was deeply concerned to encourage the search for peace in the Middle East, chaired the conference of religious leaders who went on to agree the Alexandria Declaration, which said:

> 'According to our faith traditions killing innocents in the name of God is a desecration of his Holy Name, and defames religion in the world. The violence in the Holy Land is an evil, which must be opposed by all people of good faith. We seek to live together as neighbours, respecting the integrity of each other's historical and religious inheritance. We call upon all to oppose incitement, hatred, and the misrepresentation of the other.'

The leaders called for an end to bloodshed in the name of religion and incitement against others. Signatories affirmed their respect for the other's historical and religious inheritance, and pledged to create an environment of mutual respect and trust.

Later that year Canon Andrew White – a member of CCJ – who was the Archbishop of Canterbury's representative in Bethlehem mediated the negotiations which led to the ending of the siege of the Church of the Nativity in Bethlehem, which had been occupied by militants.

CCJ also welcomed the launch by Lord Carey in 2005 of the Foundation for Reconciliation in the Middle East (FRME), which was headed at first by Canon Andrew White.

In September 2006, the Chief Rabbis of Israel, Chief Rabbi Shlomo Amar and Chief Rabbi Yonah Metzger were invited to Lambeth Palace by the Archbishop of Canterbury Dr Rowan Williams. This resulted in a Joint Declaration which committed both parties to continuing dialogue and to 'the task of peace making in the Holy Land,' of which 'the meeting today is both a sign and a potentially fruitful action to that end.'

This is the hope for which members of CCJ have prayed and worked for over 60 years.

Chapter 6. Interpreting Israel to an impatient Church

'I have to believe that peace is attainable, and that Palestinians and Israelis can live as neighbours. Why? ... Because otherwise the doubt and confusion I feel will be transformed into hatred, a hatred I see consuming too many, and I will not allow myself to go there.'

Debbie Young, CCJ Youth Officer

Telling it as it is to the British Churches.

CCJ's long term work of explaining the complex situation in Isrsael/Palestine has one aim in mind. That is to promote greater understanding and to support those working for reconciliation. CCJ has been alert to moments of crisis which might threaten good Jewish–Christian relations in Britain. There have been all too many times of sharp controversy relating to Israel/Palestine during the last twenty years.

In 1990, a delegation from the British Council of Churches briefly (for one week) visited Israel and the Occupied Territories. The group subsequently published a Report called *Impressions of Intifada.* This document 'caused great heartache to many Christians and to the Jewish community particularly.' CCJ's criticisms of the report in turn attracted criticism. An editorial in the *Church Times,* however, defended CCJ. It said 'CCJ is under criticism for being soft on Israel. The Council would be untrue to its purposes if it were not sometimes seen in this light. ... The work of CCJ is a small part of the long and penitent international effort to see that antisemitism is one day purged from the body of humankind.'

One of the authors of the report was John Dennis, the then Bishop of St Edmundsbury and Ipswich. He met with the CCJ Executive in June 1990 and explained that 'he wished the State of Israel well – he was a supporter of the State – but he felt that there were great injustices being done to the Palestinian population.' The delegation recognised Israel's need for secure boundaries.

Members of the CCJ Executive at that time felt that the delegation had not been sufficiently critical of what they were told by Palestinian Christians. In any case, it was said, they have little influence on the PLO, whose Charter, at that time, still called for the destruction of Israel. Hayim Pinner thought that Israel's human rights record compared favourably to that of the PLO itself in its dealings with Arabs who opposed it. Dr Levy, who had prepared a detailed critique of the document, said that the report had been right to say it was based on limited knowledge, and it was factually wrong and he feared a revisionist pro-Palestinian history was being developed. There was also some feeling that the report was unsympathetic to Zionism and would add to antisemitism. 'Anti-Jewish feelings are fed by such unbalanced documents.'

As so often the most balanced discussion was in the pages of *Common Ground*. In a sensitive article Rabbi Colin Eimer complained there was no mention of those Israelis who are critical of their government's policies. The report gave the impression 'that only Palestinians were concerned with peace and justice.' He objected to the sense of some 'supra-moral behaviour expected of Israel, but of Israel alone, that often forms part of the "hidden agenda" people bring with them to the region.' Colin Eimer highlighted a statement in the report 'that Israelis outrage at their own Jewish history of persecution seems not to have developed into a universal abhorrence of persecution.' 'This veiled comparison,' Colin Eimer wrote, 'between, I presume, the Holocaust and the Israeli response to the Intifada is particularly odious.' Making clear that he himself was critical of the actions of the Israeli army and of the settlers and his conviction that Israel had to make a territorial compromise, Rabbi Colin Eimer continued, 'But the remotest hint that Israeli policy is comparable to that of the Nazis makes the hackles of even the most "doveish" of Jews rise defensively. It becomes just that bit harder to listen to, and to accept, those critiques of Israeli policy which are reasonable and justified. It seems to be extremely poor taste for others, representatives of Churches which have a history of antisemitism, glibly and facilely to raise the question.'

In 1993 there was concern about the material to be used in 1994 service for the Women's World Day of Prayer, which was thought to be controversial and pro-Palestinian. In all of these cases it appears the Jewish community look to the CCJ to speak to the Christian church, to put the case for Israel. It does not expect CCJ to defend the indefensible but does call for it to speak loudly for a voice of reason and balance and to ask the church to be sensitive to Israel as well as to Palestine. For CCJ's part it too is mindful of the "slippery slope" from anti–Israel feeling born out of a frustration with the actions of some of the IDF or Israeli Government, to antisemitism.

Some in the Jewish community have felt that 'CCJ's

national profile was not good on issues' relating to Israel. Jonathan Gorsky explained, in a discussion at an Executive Committee meeting in 1995 that a lot of work was done behind the scenes. Some members felt this work needed greater publicity, so that the Jewish public could see that something was being done. Yet such publicity makes quiet diplomacy more difficult

In 2001, a report produced for the Church of England blamed the outbreak of the *Intifada* on Israel's refusal to withdraw from the 'Occupied Territories' and urged the European Union to exclude imports produced in the West Bank and Gaza from duty-free arrangements with Israel.

Anglican Call to Disinvest

In 2005 the Anglican Consultative Council (ACC), which is representative of some 77 million Anglicans across the world, called on member Churches to review their investments in companies which support 'the occupation of Palestinian lands.' The Council also welcomed a three-page statement high-lighting the 'draconian conditions' which Palestinians suffered under occupation.

The vote was condemned by some Christians, including the International Council of Christians and Jews (ICCJ) and CCJ and in articles by Clifford Longley in *The Tablet* and by Irene Lancaster in *The Church Times*. Paul Richardson of the *Church of England Newspaper* said the 'ACC should be concerned about human rights violations, including attacks on the freedom of religions, throughout the Arab world.'

The vote was widely condemned by Jews of all traditions. The Chief Rabbi was 'distressed' and Rabbi Dr Tony

Bayfield said, 'It is inconceivable that Anglican leaders don't know the pain this will cause the Jewish Community.' Both, however, were concerned to minimise the damage to Jewish-Christian friendship. The editorial in the *Jewish Chronicle* was more outspoken, objecting in particular to a report of the Anglican Peace and Justice Network (APJN), which made 'an obscene comparison between the security fence and "the barbed-wire fence of the Buchenwalt [sic] camp."' The APJN report made no mention of the fact that the wall was a response to a wave of Palestinian suicide bombings.

Melanie Phillips was even more vitriolic, saying the vote exposed the irrelevance of interfaith dialogue and particularly the ineffectiveness of the Council of Christians and Jews.' Irene Lancaster in *The Church Times* was equally critical. Her article provoked numerous letters, including one from Jane Clements on behalf of CCJ. Jane Clements recognised that some Jews felt the Anglican Consultative Council and indeed the Anglican Church were 'inherently and totally antisemitic' – a view she dismissed as 'absurd as well as offensive.' She insisted that 'Criticism of Israeli governments and concern for the plight of Palestinians is not antisemitism,' but also insisted that such criticism needed to be made with far greater sensitivity and awareness of Jewish fears. CCJ, also, at the summer conference of ICCJ, sponsored a resolution opposing disinvestments. Indeed, Sister Margaret Shepherd said that they had worked so hard on this issue that the 'criticism was hurtful.'

An article in the autumn *Common Ground* emphasised 'the need for religious institutions to be involved in peace-making rather than making hostile gestures that will only further inflame the conflict.' It explained how positive investment, more investment rather than less, can actually help both sides make progress.

The Secretary General of the Anglican Communion, Canon Kenneth Kearon, tried to diffuse the row by saying said that 'Anglicans make a clear distinction between Jewish/Christian dialogue which they value greatly, and the current policies of the Israeli government.' Perhaps after the controversy, he realised that many Jews do not recognise that distinction and honest dialogue cannot put 'Israel' in brackets

Following this call from the Anglican Consultative Council an attempt was made by some members of the General Synod of the Church of England to persuade the advisory body on the Church's investments to withdraw its shares from Caterpillar, which manufactures bulldozers. This was because, it was claimed, such equipment sold by the company to Israel had been used in the demolition of Palestinian homes. The Church Commissioners, however, decided not to act on the Synod's vote in favour of this disinvestment.

In 2007, once again, there was concern about Christian Aid's stance on the Israel-Palestine situation. It was agreed that CCJ should prepare Position Statements on important topics such as antisemitism and Israel, which are still available today.

A Private Member's motion at the meeting of General Synod in July 2012 calling for support for the Ecumenical Accompaniment Programme (EAPPI), which sends human-rights monitors to observe check points in Israel again provoked angry debate.

Methodist Call for a Boycott

In 2010 the Methodist Church became embroiled in a similar row. In June, its Annual Conference, meeting in Portsmouth, voted as a Church to boycott all products from Israeli (so-called 'illegal') settlements in Palestinian territories and encouraged Methodists across Britain to do the same. In doing so, it was responding to a call by the World Council of Churches for an 'international boycott of settlement produce and services.' The decision was part of a long resolution, which also denounced the Separation Barrier, the blockade of Gaza, and visa restrictions on Palestinians, as well as calling for an arms embargo. The Resolution also referred to the much-criticised UN Goldstone report that accused both Israelis and Palestinians of war crimes during the Gaza Operation.

Prior to the vote, members of Conference had been circulated with a fifty-four page report, which only made a passing reference to Hamas, and which critics said was 'full of basic historical inaccuracies, deliberate misrepresentation and distortions of Jewish theology and Israeli policy.'

There was a furious reaction from the Jewish community. The Board of Deputies cut all links with the Methodist Church. The Jewish Leadership Council said the Methodist Conference should 'hang its head in shame.' The Chief Rabbi, Lord Sacks, said the accompanying report showed 'no genuine understanding of one of the most complex conflicts in the world today' and that the vote would damage the 'hitherto harmonious relationship between the faith communities in the UK.' Others used stronger language. Geoffrey Alderman said the report was 'a philosophy of utter contempt for Jews and Judaism' and claimed that one of the authors of the report spoke of the Jewish view of God as 'a racist God who has favourites.' Alderman went on to say that the vote showed the futility of interfaith work.

If those who are not living in Israel-Palestine and have not mourned the death of family members in the conflict so obviously cannot hear what the other side is saying, it is the more amazing that there are any peace moves in the Middle East.

CCJ had warned the Methodist Church that the report and resolution were flawed and likely to cause great consternation and reaction in the Jewish community. All CCJ's local branches were asked to engage with local Methodist groups so as to encourage Methodists 'to listen to the other side.' David Gifford said 'The Jewish community is very hurt. The report and the resolutions could clearly impact on Britain's Jewish community.' He added that it would take time to repair the damage.

David Gifford also wrote to the *Jewish Chronicle*. 'The Methodist Church's motion on Israel was ill-advised, misguided and potentially counter-productive… The call for a boycott of goods and services from the occupied territories will have a damaging effect on those on all sides who seek peace, dialogue and tolerance.' He went on to say that Jews should not forget the 'massive goodwill' of many Christians and insisted that 'rather than showing the futility of interfaith work, the events had highlighted its importance.' A number of Methodists were highly critical of the Conference resolutions, whereas Richard Kuper of 'Jews for Justice for Palestinians' congratulated the Conference and as a supporter of 'Peace and Reconciliation' cheered 'from the side-lines.'

Not just through its branches but behind the scenes the CCJ was working for reconciliation. Dr Lionel Kopelowitz, a CCJ Vice President and a former President of the Board of Deputies, met privately with senior members of the Methodist Church to listen to their views and to explain the British Jewish community's feelings on the Report. Eventually, thanks to the efforts of CCJ, relations between the Board of Deputies of British Jews and the Methodist Church have been restored with regular meetings between the leaders of the Methodist Church and the Board of Deputies. There followed some comment that the CCJ should convene these future meetings between the two parties. CCJ resisted this and felt its mediatory role was fulfilled in this case and that the Methodist Church and The Board of Deputies now had a restored trust enabling their own conversations. CCJ had however also gained credence in the Jewish community by its public statements, although it may have lost the backing of some Christians.

Again in late 2011, some of the Trustees of the Churches Together in Britain and Ireland (CTBI) made a study visit to Israel and the occupied Territories. Their report whilst containing some encouraging perspectives was not uncritical of Israeli responses in several areas. To avoid a repeat of the Methodist Church Report the previous year, CCJ invited CTBI and the Board of Deputies of British Jews to meet and discuss the Report before it went public. This offer was taken up with a further invitation from the CTBI for the Board of Deputies to upload its comments and responses on CTBI's own website. This was seen by many to be indicative of an improved state of Jewish-Christian understanding.

Supporting the Search for Peace and Justice

With such a variety of views how can the Council of Christians and Jews be representative of all Christians and Jews? It cannot. Members of both communities need to recognise the divisions within each community. Although CCJ has strong backing from the British religious leaders who are its Presidents, it is an independent voluntary organisation – not a Council with officially appointed delegates. Its task is to try to interpret each community to the other and provide channels of communication.

Members of CCJ - whether Jewish or Christian - are firmly committed to Israel's right to exist and support its people. This does not mean that they are uncritical of some policies of the Israeli government or the actions of some members of the security forces or settlers in the West Bank. In 1995, at the April meeting of the Executive, Mrs Beryl Norman expressed concern about the Israeli government's treatment of ex-patriate Christians, with specific reference to the non-renewal of visas. At the September meeting in the same year, David Craig said that some people were having difficulty going to their holy places. It was agreed that a letter should be sent to the Israeli ambassador.

Jonathan Gorsky, as CCJ's Deputy Education Officer, has on several occasions courageously challenged the hard-line views of some in the Jewish community, emphasising the human tragedy of the conflict. 'The impact of military confrontation is profound and painful.' he wrote, 'Young men, who were but school boys a few years ago ...hurt by pelting stones and stung by abusive taunts ...over-react ... The memory of lost friends overwhelms their sense of decency.' 'When we pray for the peace of the Holy Land we must hear the narratives of Israelis and of Palestinians and help each to listen to the other, so dispelling images of conflict and violence and slowly creating a new and more promising reality. Israelis and Palestinians are people, just as we are, with families, children, hopes, sorrows, joys and aspirations. Their lives are distorted by an embattled and violent political context and we must pursue peace with understanding, patience and great sensitivity to the experience of both societies.

Again in 2002, while recognising Israeli anger at the Palestinian rejection of the far-reaching concessions offered by Prime Minister Barak and the subsequent violence, Jonathan Gorsky reminded readers that 'it is surely one of the great lessons of the Biblical narratives that even in waging a just war we are in great jeopardy ... In war and in conflict we lose sight of the humanity of the other; we too become capable of terrible things and our own humanity becomes very fragile indeed.'

In another article entitled 'Unto Thy Seed I Will Give This Land,' Jonathan Gorsky gave a critical account of the Settlement Movement. 'The settlements,' he wrote 'continue to have a drastic impact on both Palestinians and Israeli politics, with the Palestinians further embittered and inflamed by the overwhelming trials of their daily existence and the Israeli security barrier which has encroached on yet more Palestinian land.' Jonathan Gorsky argued that all this had weakened the efforts of moderate Palestinians and had played into the hands of Hamas. He also stated that half of Israelis wanted the settlement project to end. 'Religious leaders,' he said, 'must take their courage in both hands and make statements that will be highly unpopular, but might ultimately rekindle the politics of hope. It is possible and necessary for the Israelis and Palestinians to live together. The alternative is quite unthinkable.'

There was a sharp reply in the following issue of *Common Ground* by Avi Cohen, an Israeli journalist. 'I wholly disagree with his argument that the "settlement project" bears responsibility for the violence and terrorism of the Intifada… The Hamas Charter … makes it quite clear that it seeks to eradicate the Jewish State as a whole… Even if there were no Jews at all on the West Bank or in Gaza and Israel returned to the pre-1967 borders, Hamas would still be waging Jihad on the Jewish State and terrorism would still be seen as legitimate.'

In times of armed conflict, such as the battles with Hezbollah on the Lebanon border or fighting in Gaza, outsiders, including CCJ can do little. They can urge restraint; make clear that Israel only resorts to an armed response in the face of prolonged provocation and try to ensure that the hostility is not replicated in relations between the faith communities in Britain.

It has been important to discuss times of tension in some detail as they highlight the complex task that CCJ undertakes. Boycotts and denunciations may make the boycotters feel virtuous, they do little to progress the agonizingly slow peace-building that is in the long term interest of both Israelis and Palestinians.

Chapter 7 . Mission

'What we need is an entente cordiale ... in which both religions would offer the best they have to each other.'
Reinhold Niebuhr

If Israel's security is non-negotiable for many Jews, the call to mission is non-negotiable for many Christians. Christians associated with CCJ would certainly repudiate 'proselytism' in the sense of high-pressure evangelism and targeting of Jews. Christians, however, even if they interpret it in different ways, cannot forget the 'Great Commission' of the Risen Jesus 'to go and make disciples of all nations, baptising them in the name of the Father and of the Son and of the Holy Spirit, and teaching them to obey everything I have commanded.' For Jews, however, attempts by Christians to convert them imply that the 'New Covenant' has replaced the 'Old Covenant' and that therefore their religion, in Christian eyes, is inferior and out-dated. Mission also brings back bitter memories of forced conversions, pogroms and persecution.

CCJ has always made it clear that it is not a missionary body. CCJ has consistently opposed coercive or deceitful evangelism and has strongly objected to 'targeting of Jews.' Even if evangelism is an appropriate activity for Christians today, focussing on one particular group is distasteful. This is one reason why George Carey, when he became Archbishop of Canterbury, declined to become a patron of CMJ (The Church's Ministry among Jewish People). In his letter to CMJ, he said that he wished to build up the trust of the Jewish community. He could not, therefore, be closely associated with an organization 'entirely directed towards another faith community.' Lord Carey felt it was contradictory for him to be both a Joint President of CCJ and a Patron of CMJ.

This position statement on 'Mission, Evangelism and Proselytising' outlines CCJ's approach to this sensitive topic:

> Christianity is based on an understanding of the loving engagement of God with humanity through the life, death and resurrection of Jesus. It is the responsibility of Christians to witness in their lives to the good news of this mission of God in the ways that Jesus did – by lives of love in action. Christian members of CCJ will therefore want to focus on serving others and witnessing to their faith through deeds and dialogue… Christians who seek to convert Jews do so because they sincerely believe it to be in the best interests of all Jews, without any intention to cause distress. However, throughout the difficult history of Christian-Jewish relations, there have been continuing attempts to persuade or force Jews to convert and to abandon their Jewish identity. Jews then and now feel that Christian enthusiasm for targeting them for conversion stems from a lack of respect for Judaism as a religion. The tragic history of Christian treatment of Jews in many parts of Europe means that Jews see missionary approaches as a reminder of past suffering and they are therefore hurt and upset by this. Many of us make 'journeys of faith' within our own traditions. Sometimes, individuals may cross boundaries. However, proselytising – that is "aggressive

and manipulative attempts to convert" completely contradicts everything that CCJ values, namely respecting and encouraging the traditions and identities of each other, seeking to learn and share, to encourage our own faith and practice.

'Jewish Christians'

CCJ has been especially critical of the activities of 'Jews for Jesus,' which is one of the most high-profile movements of 'Messianic Jews'. This group's advertising campaigns in several newspapers and on the underground attracted particular criticism.

The very phrase 'Jewish Christian' is controversial. Most members of the Jewish community do not regard those who belong to another religion as still being Jews, even if they are Jewish by birth - as for them being Jewish is a matter of faith as well as birth.

Some Jews who have converted to Christianity join mainstream churches. Hugh Montefiore, who described himself as 'Jewish Christian,' became a bishop of the Church of England, but felt excluded from CCJ. Others who call themselves 'Hebrew Christians' have been active members of CCJ.

The position of those who call themselves 'Messianic Jews' is the most problematic. The term is used by people who are Jewish by birth and who believe that Yeshua (Jesus) is the promised Jewish Messiah. Often they will worship on the Sabbath and use Hebrew.

This issue came to a head in 1994, when the late Paul

Mendel, at that time Director of the CCJ, reported to the Executive that some members of the Messianic Foundation were taking part in the Brighton and Hove branch and that one of the branch officers was involved. 'It was felt that it is incompatible for an officer of a CCJ branch to be a supporter of such groups.' A working party was set up but, because of the complexity of the subject, a Code of Practice was not produced until the summer of 1996, which said:

> 1. In the past fifty years Christian-Jewish relations have made great progress. Important theological statements by respective religious leaders have been accompanied by warmth, friendship and supportive personal contact at every level. After a long and sometimes tragic history these developments are profoundly moving. CCJ exists to nurture and promote this new relationship between Christian and Jews.
>
> 2. Insensitive comments about Christianity or Judaism, or attempts to use CCJ for missionary activity destroy the mutual trust that is essential to our work. Dialogue must be guided by an understanding of the depth and sensitivities of religious commitment, as well as a knowledge of the historical experiences of Christian and Jewish communities.
>
> 3. In the event of failure to respect these sensitivities, branch committees must ensure that the people concerned understand and agree to abide by this code of practice in future. If such efforts are to no avail, then, after consultation with Head Office, privileges of membership will be withdrawn.

4. If representatives of either Christian or Jewish communities inform the local branch committee of hurtful behaviour by a CCJ member, then the matter must be looked into, and reported to Head Office.

5. Aggressive proselytism is always wrong and if this or any unsuitable behaviour is reported to CCJ, appropriate action will be taken. Concern will not be confined to behaviour within CCJ.

6. Every effort must be made to achieve a reconciliation. Forfeiture of membership will be a last resort.

The *Jewish Chronicle* and the *Church Times* gave the Code of Practice a favourable reception, although Dan Cohn-Sherbok's article in the *Church of England Newspaper* was critical. Members mostly supported the Code of Practice, although there were a few resignations. The *Jewish Chronicle's* Editorial was headed 'Wise Council.'

The reaction of large sections of the Jewish community to the Council of Christians and Jews is either indifference or suspicion. The indifference is born either of ignorance of the work the Council does or a failure to appreciate the value of the work. The suspicion is that Christians who participate in CCJ activities do so with the ultimate purpose of trying to convert Jews. Both attitudes are to be deplored. With the Chief Rabbi and the heads of all major churches as its president, the Council is an important body which, in theory at least, can swing into action whenever religion or religious beliefs are under attack. At grass-roots level, it enables members of its branches up and down the country, and abroad, too to learn about the beliefs and practices of each other's religion – and Christian ignorance of Judaism is matched only by Jewish ignorance of Christianity

Some Jews find it hard to accept that there are non-Jews who really do admire Judaism *per se* and want to have friendly and meaningful relations with its adherents ...

That the leadership of CCJ which includes the Archbishops of Canterbury and Westminster has seen fit this week to issue a code of practice to all its branches stressing the inadmissibility of missionary activity under the cloak of interfaith work is to be welcomed. But as with many other initiatives, the test will come if and when the code of practice has to be implemented by expelling anyone found guilty of contravening it. In the meantime, the mere fact that is has been issued is reason enough for Jewish sceptics who have kept their distance from the Council to come forward and strengthen it. There is little point in decrying its weaknesses if the very people - particularly religious leaders - who could give it muscle stay away from it.

Should Christians seek for the Conversion of Jews?

CCJ has always made clear that its meetings should not be used for 'conversionist' activity. The question of mission itself is more far reaching. Should Christians still seek the conversion of Jews?

Decade of Evangelism
The issue came to the fore when the Church of England decided to launch a Decade of Evangelism to prepare for the

Millennium. This created much anxiety among the Jewish community and among many Christian members of CCJ. 'Mission' was a subject much discussed at meetings of the Executive Committee, in *Common Ground* and at the Hengrave Hall Conference.

An editorial in *Common Ground* suggested that the idea of the Decade 'sent a shiver down the spine of some Christians as well as members of other faiths.' It said that although sharing the good news might seem harmless enough, too often in the past 'preaching the Gospel had been accompanied by threats.' The editorial called instead for 'shared witness' to the ethical and religious values held in common by Judaism and Christianity. It pointed out that 'the Ten Commandments, whilst revealed to Israel, are applicable to all people.'

Church leaders did their best to assure Jews that they would not be 'targeted.' There was further discussion of the Decade of Evangelism at the February 1991 Executive. It was recognised that CCJ could not stop the Churches' involvement in mission, as they were missionary by nature and calling, but it could question methods of missionary activities. At a subsequent meeting Lord Coggan presented a paper on the subject. A CCJ statement on the Decade emphasised the importance of dialogue.

At a subsequent meeting of the Executive, Rabbi Hugo Gryn objected to the name 'Spearhead' being used of the next stage of the Decade as the same title was used by an extreme right-wing magazine. As a result of a letter sent by Michael Latham to Lambeth Palace, the name of next stage of the Decade was changed to 'Springboard.'

The 1994 Hengrave Hall CCJ Conference was on Mission. There was a rather defensive talk by Canon Philip King, (then) General Secretary of the Board of Mission of the General Synod of the Church of England. David Blewett, who was a full-time consultant on Christian-Jewish relations in the USA, however, made clear his objection to "Jewish evangelism," by which he meant evangelism to Jewish people. 'I once supported Jewish evangelism, but I now strongly oppose it because it assumes that God's covenant with Abraham has been replaced with a better one … The proselytising of Jews will end only when we (Christians) realise that Jews are born into an unconditional covenant relationship.' An unusual contribution came from John Launer, who applied his skills as a family therapist. Instead of arguments about who started it, the family therapist looks to new possibilities. He concluded, 'Jews have always needed Christians to further the universalist mission. Christians have always needed Jews to sustain the pure and moral monotheism of their founder.'

Jane Clements, the Education Officer, in an article in *Common Ground* suggested that Evangelical Christian leaders should encourage a more critical reading of scripture and emphasise the 'social gospel' and 'the universality of God'

Different Approaches

Christians are by no means agreed on the meaning of mission. Leading Anglican members of CCJ have taken an active part in this often heated theological debate about what is meant by mission and whether Christians should pray for and seek the conversion of Jews. It is important, therefore at least in outline to identify the key issues in the debate, which relate to the radical rethinking of the Church's relation to Judaism, which CCJ has done so much to encourage. We shall look at Roman Catholic teaching on this subject in the chapter on Catholic-Jewish Relations.

There are broadly three approaches, which one could summarise as 'Seek Converts'; 'Introduce Jesus'; and 'Co-witness.' These are set out rather more fully in *Christians and Jews: A New Way of Thinking,* produced by a working group which was chaired by Bishop Richard Harries. They were echoed in the subsequent report *Sharing One Hope.* The three positions are:

> 1. It is not appropriate for Christians to believe that they have any kind of 'Mission to the Jews.'

> 2. It is entirely appropriate that Christians who establish relations of genuine friendship and trust with Jews should continue to see these relationships in the context of Christian mission.

> 3. Christians have a responsibility to try to convince Jews about Jesus as Messiah.

We will consider them in reverse order.

Conversion

Many Christians - although they are unlikely to be members of CCJ - hold to the third option: the hope that Jews will come to faith in Jesus Christ. In 2008, for example, the World Evangelical Alliance (WEA) urged its members to renew 'their commitment to the task of Jewish evangelism.' This was supported by its British affiliate, the Evangelical

Alliance (EA). After the usual cautions, the document says 'Christians everywhere must not look away when Jewish people have the same deep need for forgiveness of sin and true shalom, as do people of all nations. Love in action compels all Christians to share the gospel with people everywhere, including the Jewish people of Europe.' David Gifford, Chief Executive of CCJ, was quoted as saying that it was time for the Evangelical Alliance to 'move on' and recognise modern theological thinking which accepts 'the validity of the Jewish faith and its relationship with God.'

Introducing Jesus

The second position of 'introducing Jesus' would find considerable support among Christian members of CCJ. Soon after the launch of the Decade of Evangelism, Lord Coggan, as mentioned above, was invited to address the subject at a meeting of the Executive Committee. He acknowledged the unease of the Jewish community about the Decade of Evangelism. In lecturing to theological students, he said, he reminded them that in the first century Jews in the Diaspora witnessed to their faith and attracted many Gentiles as 'God-fearers.' There was nothing wrong with mission *per se*. He also pointed out that 'evangel' just meant 'Good News' – but was distorted when '-ism' was added to make it 'Evange<u>lism</u>.' Lord Coggan deplored 'proselytism,' which implied 'arm-twisting' or 'spiritual rape'- seen at its worst in American TV evangelism. It also undermined Jewish trust, which had, in any case, been sorely damaged by the 'horror' of Jewish/Christian history. On the other hand, Christians would not gain Jewish respect by never mentioning Jesus. 'We offer and commend, because we love and share.' In conclusion Lord Coggan reiterated a point he often made that Jews and Christians need to witness together to the values that they share to the pagan society in which we live.

Archbishop George Carey, a strong supporter of CCJ, questioned the view that there are two parallel covenants – one for Jews and one Christians – and that therefore Christians should not try to convert Jews. 'I do not abandon the desire to introduce Jewish friends to my faith and the way I see it.'

Cardinal William Kasper, President of the Pontifical Council for promoting Christian Unity, as we shall see, took a similar position in a carefully nuanced lecture. He included in it a section on mission. Despite all the emphasis on caution and sensitivity he made clear 'that Christians and the church are generally required to give Jews witness to their faith in Jesus Christ now.'

Shared Witness

A vocal proponent of the first view that attempts to convert Jews are inappropriate is Richard Harries, former Bishop of Oxford and a former Chairman of CCJ. 'Can I pray that my Jewish friends are converted to Christianity? My honest answer is no.' Richard Harries in his book *After the Evil*, explains the reasons for his answer. He rejects the view that Christianity is just 'Judaism for the Gentiles,' because there are real differences. Yet the two religions live in inescapable partnership with one another. He then goes on to affirm five points. 'First, Judaism is a living religion through which Jews relate to the one true living God…Secondly, the voice or language of Judaism preserves precious insights which it is important not to lose... Thirdly, Jews understandably see conversion to Christianity as both a betrayal and a loss of identity... Fourthly, in the light of the long history of the teaching of contempt, the Christian Church is called to repent... Fifthly, Christians and Jews share a common mission.'

Many members of CCJ would be sympathetic to Richard Harries' arguments, but as an organisation CCJ has to allow for a variety of views amongst both its Jewish and its Christian members. The theological debate on the understanding of Christian mission is one for the Churches. Its intricacies may seem arcane to most Jews, but they are important as they show the very marked shift in Christian teaching and behaviour in the last fifty years. It may not go far enough for many Jews and for some Christians, but the real progress to which CCJ's Christian members have made a major contribution should be widely welcomed. It is right for CCJ to make the issues known to a wider public and help them appreciate the diversity of views and the reasons for them. By encouraging meeting and conversation, CCJ ensures that the theological debate is grounded in the realities of dialogue and active co-operation.

The Jewish Mission

The focus has been on Christian mission, but in the centuries before the dominance of Christianity and Islam, whole nations were converted to Judaism and many Gentiles became 'God-fearers.' The Lambeth-Jewish Forum, which includes rabbis and Anglican clergymen, some of whom are active members of the CCJ, took two to three years to explore the concept of mission from a Jewish and Christian perspective. Rabbi Reuvan Silverman, in the first part of a book produced by the Forum, left the reader in no doubt that from the time of Abraham, the Jewish faith had a strong mission element contained in the Covenants.

The mission of Jews today - or in the words of Joint President Rabbi Tony Bayfield, 'the Jewish purpose in life' - 'is to live out the spiritual and ethical paradigm that the Torah frames and teaches ... The fidelity is not merely for its own sake but should radiate blessing and enlightenment far beyond the family of Israel.'

Rabbi Bayfield ended his article with these words: 'The route to the day on which "God will be One and God's name One" lies not through mission as conquest or conversion but through mission as the full realization in each Jew, Christian and Muslim of the best that each of the Abrahamic faiths can teach. In that way and only in that way is the ultimate redemption that we all yearn for, made possible.'

Chapter 8. Catholic-Jewish Relations

'A new beginning destined to overcome centuries of misunderstanding, enmity and even hatred and persecution'
Gerhard Reigner on 'Nostra Aetate'

Why a special chapter on Catholic-Jewish relations? Members of the Free Churches, of the Church of Scotland, of the Anglican Church, as well as Roman Catholics, have all contributed to a new appreciation of Judaism and closer relations with the Jewish community.

There are several reasons. The first is that nearly half of the Christians in the world are Catholics and often a majority in countries where there was or is a sizeable Jewish population. Secondly, the Vatican is a sovereign state with diplomatic relations with other countries and a presence at the United Nations. Thirdly Vatican statements and the words and actions of the Pope have a bearing on Christian-Jewish relations in Britain and in many other parts of the world and are therefore very relevant to the work of CCJ. Fourthly, there have also been regular meetings with the International Jewish Committee for Interreligious Consultations, whereas the World Council of Churches has evaded the subject at its Assemblies lest the debate were to be hijacked by anti-Zionists, although some of the member churches of World Council of Churches have issued relevant statements.

Revising the teaching of the Roman Catholic Church.

The decree *Nostra Aetate*, 'In Our Age', promulgated in October 1965 by the Second Vatican Council, was a decisive turning point not only in Catholic-Jewish relations, but also more broadly for Christian-Jewish relations. *Nostra Aetate* began by recalling the spiritual bond that links the people of the New Covenant to Abraham's stock and by affirming God's continuing covenant with the Jewish people. The document commended dialogue. Most important, the charge of deicide was repudiated. The decree also condemned all persecution and particularly displays of antisemitism. In 2005 a seminar to mark the fortieth anniversary of *Nostra Aetate* was held, arranged jointly by CCJ with the Sisters of Sion.

In the years since *Nostra Aetate*, the new approach has been amplified in various Vatican documents such as:

We Remember: a Reflection on the Shoah (1998) was an expression of the Church's repentance for those Christians who failed to oppose Nazi persecution of the Jews. It produced mixed reactions and some criticism from Jews who felt it did not go far enough. Bishop Henderson reminded members of the CCJ Executive that the statement was primarily addressed to Roman Catholics.

'The Jewish People and Their Sacred Scriptures in the Christian Bible' (2002) acknowledged that 'the horror in the wake of the extermination of the Jews (the Shoah) during the Second World War had led all the Churches to rethink their relationship with Judaism and, as a

result, to reconsider their interpretation of the Jewish Bible, the Old Testament.' The document said that 'Christians can and ought to admit that the Jewish reading of the Bible is a possible one.' It also says that 'Without the Old Testament, the New Testament would be an incomprehensible book.' The document, however, clearly rejects the suggestion that there is any real anti-Jewish feeling in the New Testament.

A particularly creative moment in Catholic-Jewish Dialogue was the Millennium Conference at the Sternberg Centre in May 2000. This brought together eminent Catholic and Jewish scholars. *He Kissed Him and They Wept.* Is the record of their deliberations Although the conference was not arranged by CCJ, a significant number of the participants were active members of CCJ.

Pope John Paul II

Pope John Paul II, or Karol Wojtyla (to give him his birth name) grew up in Wadowice, a Polish town with a population of 8,000 Catholics and 2,000 Jews. His childhood friendship with Jerzy Kluger continued even while he was Pope. John Paul II was well aware of the deep sufferings of the Jewish People. He was personally committed to working for better relationships.

There were many "firsts" during his Papacy. He was the first Pope to visit the Rome Synagogue. He was also the first Pope to make an official and historic visit to Israel. This was in 2000, the year of the Christian Millennium. At the Western Wall Pope John Paul II placed a prayer asking

God's forgiveness for any way in which Christians 'had caused your children to suffer.' 'The image of the elderly Pontiff praying at the Western Wall in Jerusalem, requesting forgiveness for the suffering of the Jewish people was deeply moving, opening Israeli eyes in particular to a changed reality. The Church was no longer the enemy.'

Common Ground devoted several pages to this historic event including what the Pope said at Yad Vashem and Prime Minister Ehud Barak's response.

The Pope made clear his deep sadness at 'the hatred, acts of persecution and displays of antisemitism directed against Jews by Christians at any time and in any place. The Church rejects racism in any form as a denial of the image of the Creator inherent in every human being.' The Prime Minister ended his reply with the words, 'Your Holiness, you have come on a mission of brotherhood, of remembrance, of peace. And we say to you: Blessed are you in Israel.' CCJ itself, at an event in the Durbar Court at the Foreign Office, presented a plaque to the Papal Nuncio to commemorate the Pope's pilgrimage.

Pope John Paul II also showed an interest in the work of CCJ. A highlight of 1991 was the visit to the Vatican of a CCJ delegation consisting of Edward Carpenter, Sir Sigmund Sternberg – wearing the uniform of a papal knight – Sidney Corob, Bishop Mahon and Jim Richardson. They were granted an audience with the Pope and paid a courtesy call on the then Italian Prime Minister. Later a Young Leaders' visit to Rome included a private audience with the Pope.

The death of Pope John Paul II in 2005 highlighted the dramatic changes in Christian-Jewish relations since the Vatican II's ground-breaking decree *Nostra Aetate,* forty years earlier. Pope John Paul II did more than any church leader to create a brotherly relationship between Catholics and Jews. The year before the Pope died, Bishop Christopher Herbert, Chairman of CCJ, was granted an audience with the Pope. Shortly before Pope John Paul II's death more than 100 rabbis, cantors and other Jewish leaders journeyed to Rome, for a private audience, at which they thanked him for all his efforts in this field. Gary Krupp, the president and founder of 'Pave the Way' said to him 'You have defended the Jewish people at every opportunity, as a priest in Poland and during your pontificate.' In reply Pope John Paul II said, 'May this be an occasion for renewed commitment to increased understanding and co-operation in the service of building a world ever more firmly based on respect for the divine image in every human being.' The Israeli Government commemorated his death by issuing special stamps on what would have been his eighty-fifth birthday.

Pope Benedict XVI

Pope Benedict XVI's relations with the Jewish people have been more difficult, not least because he grew up in Nazi Germany. Moreover his theology is more traditional. He holds that all salvation ultimately depends upon the sacrifice of Christ, which is mediated to people through the Catholic Church. He accepts, however, that there are those outside the Church who receive that grace, without knowing its source. Pope Benedict XVI has always maintained the position that we can only speak of a single covenant linking Jews and Christians.

Professor John Pawlikowsi, a Roman Catholic theologian who was a former President of the International Council of Christians and Jews, has said that for Pope Benedict, 'Any talk of dual covenants is tantamount to heresy... Pre-eschatologically (that is before last days) there exist two different paths. Ratzinger clearly affirms that the Jewish community advances to final salvation through continuing obedience to its revealed covenantal tradition. In the end Christ will confirm that Jewish covenant. Thus Christ remains central to ultimate Jewish salvation, though it is not fully clear whether Ratzinger believes Jews must explicitly acknowledge Christ to attain full salvation.'

A fuller explanation of the Catholic position was given by Cardinal William Kasper, who was President of the Pontifical Council for Promoting Christian Unity. In a carefully nuanced lecture he included a section on Mission. It showed the cautious way in which Church teaching is being modified, but also made clear 'that Christians and the Church are generally required to give Jews witness to their faith in Jesus Christ now,' as this extract shows:

> 'There is a differentiation between the two religions that is neither a simple parallel co-existence, nor an opposition... Judaism and Christianity need each other. A well thought-out determination of the relationship of Israel and the Church is fundamental to answering the highly controversial question of Christian mission among the Jews. This is for Jews a very delicate and sensitive question, because it has implications for the existence of Israel itself. But the question is delicate also

for Christians, because the universal salvific significance of Jesus Christ and the universal mission of the Church are fundamental for Christian belief. Also Paul on his missionary journeys went always first (Romans 1,16) to the Jews in the synagogue, and only after he met opposition, did he turn to the Gentiles. So as Christians we can and must recognize that this universality can and must be applied in different ways to pagans and to Jews. Jews are not pagans, they believe in one God and have therefore not to turn from false and dead idols to the true and living God (I Thessalonians 1, 9). This means that the command for mission is as valid for Jews as for pagans but it must be put into effect differently among Jews than with respect to pagans.

This difference has not always been observed, and unfortunately there has been a history of forced conversions of Jews. In principle, though, and especially today the church takes this difference into account. In contrast to some fundamentalist evangelical movements which undertake missionary work, the Catholic Church has no specific institutional missionary work aimed at Jews. This is more than a mere fact; it is an important ecclesial reality. This does not mean that the church and Christians should behave passively in the meantime and simply sit on their hands. The exclusion of a targeted institutional mission does not prohibit, but rather implies that Christians and the church are generally required to give Jews witness to their faith in Jesus Christ now.'

Cardinal Kasper insisted that witness should be 'discreet and humble' and should, especially after the Shoah, avoid triumphalism. He recognised that some Jews may choose to become Christians and some Christians to become Jews. He concluded this section of his lecture by saying, 'the salvation of all Israel is according Saint Paul left to God alone at the end of time (Romans 11, 26ff). In this sense the Pontifical Biblical Commission says: "Jewish messianic expectation is not in vain"; at the end of time both Jews and Christians will recognize the "One who is to come" (the eschatological messiah).

Despite being more theologically conservative than his predecessor, Pope Benedict XVI has followed his predecessor's example in visiting the Rome Synagogue, in meeting Jewish leaders wherever he travels and in journeying to Israel.

At Yad Vashem, after laying a wreath, he said the suffering of Holocaust victims must never be denied. 'May the names of these victims never perish. May their suffering never be denied, belittled or forgotten.' He also shook the hands of six Holocaust survivors before making a sombre speech about the six million Jews killed in the Shoah 'They lost their lives, but they will never lose their names,' he said. 'These are indelibly etched in the hearts of their loved ones, their surviving fellow prisoners and all those determined never to allow such an atrocity to disgrace mankind again.'

At the end of his visit to the Holy Land, Pope Benedict made a heartfelt plea for peace. 'No more bloodshed, no more fighting, no more terrorism, no more war.' He reiterated the call for a two-state solution, as Israel had the right to exist, and the Palestinians 'have a right to a sovereign independent homeland'. He also spoke about the wall built by Israeli authorities to separate Israel from Palestinian territories. 'As I passed alongside it, I prayed for a future in which the peoples of the Holy Land can live together in peace and harmony without the need for such instruments of security and separation.'

Strained Relations

Despite the progress of the last twenty years, there have been times of tension, often due to lack of sensitivity and a clash of symbols.

<u>The Carmelite Convent at Auschwitz</u>

Both were evident in the distressing controversy surrounding the Carmelite Convent at Auschwitz. A few Barefoot Carmelite nuns had in 1984 set up a small convent in a building known as the 'Old Theatre' on the perimeter of Auschwitz. Subsequently in 1989, some Belgian Catholics raised money for them 'to guarantee the conversion of strayed brothers.' Many in the Jewish world reacted strongly both against the implied attempt to convert Jews and to impose Christian symbols on a place of special remembrance for Jews. Eventually the nuns moved to a non-controversial site.

In 1990, Rabbi Dr Norman Solomon wrote of the controversy: No one 'had paused to ask the meaning of the phrase, "conversion of strayed brother" which sounded alarm bells in the Jewish world. But what raises our hackles is (to spell out the emotion) the building of nunneries on the graves of our murdered brethren, the imposition of a

Christian presence where it is least appropriate. There is a clash of symbols here, and where symbols clash there is no reconciliation but an aggravation of the wound.'

The Canonisation of Edith Stein

The Canonisation of Edith Stein was also a clash of symbols. Edith Stein (1891-1942) was the youngest child of a Jewish family in Breslau. She converted to Catholicism in 1922 and entered the Carmelite convent in Cologne in 1933. Arrested by the Gestapo, she was sent to Auschwitz and murdered there on arrival. To Catholics she was a martyr – but did she die for her Christian faith or because she was born a Jew? 'Whether she saw Jews in the Holocaust as witnessing to the persecuted Christ or as a sacrifice for their own sins, clearly neither view voiced by a convert to Christianity coincides with Jewish self-understanding … Some commentators saw the Catholic Church's beatification of Stein as a confirmation of her interpretation of Jews in negative supersessionist terms and consequently as a step backwards in Jewish-Christian relations.'

The proposed beatification of Pope Pius XII

The proposed beatification of Pope Pius XII has also disturbed members of the Jewish community, because it was felt in some quarters that his resistance to Hitler had been inadequate. The historical evidence is disputed and the issue remains a matter of continuing controversy.

The Passion of the Christ,

Mel Gibson's film *The Passion of the Christ*, released in 2004, caused some consternation because of its violence and its outdated and negative views of Jews and Judaism and its selective use of scripture. The German bishops and *The Tablet*, a British Catholic weekly, were critical and feared the film might revive discarded anti-Jewish teaching. It was a reminder how easily Christians slip back into their old way of thinking.

Holocaust Denial: Bishop Williamson

CCJ has joined with others in strongly opposing all forms of Holocaust denial. This was why the Roman Catholic bishops in Britain were forthright in denouncing the views of Bishop Richard Williamson of the Society of St Pius X. This society, founded by Archbishop Marcel Lefebvre, attracted a small group of traditional Roman Catholics who objected to the reforms of the Second Vatican Council. They were excommunicated by the then Pope. Pope Benedict XVI in an act of 'paternal mercy' lifted their excommunication. He hoped that this together with the reintroduction of the Tridentine Rite, would enable Traditionalists to be reconciled to the Church. One of the bishops whose excommunication was lifted was Richard Williamson – a known Holocaust denier. Was the Pope ignorant of this or did he choose to ignore it? In the face a furious response from many Jewish leaders, the Vatican quickly distanced itself from Bishop Williamson's views.

The Catholic Bishops in Britain immediately said that Bishop Williamson's views were 'totally unacceptable.' They called on all Roman Catholics to deplore antisemitism in all its forms.

The Good Friday Prayer for the Jews.

The traditional Roman Catholic Good Friday prayer for the Jews called for their conversion.

(For the conversion of Jews:) Let us pray also for the Jews that the Lord our God may take the veil from their hearts and that they also may acknowledge our Lord Jesus Christ. (Let us pray:) Almighty and everlasting God, you do not refuse your mercy even to the Jews; hear the prayers which we offer for the blindness of that people so that they may acknowledge the light of your truth, which is Christ, and be delivered from their darkness.

In 1970, as a result of the new approach to Jews, following the Second Vatican Council, the prayer was significantly altered to read:

Let us pray for the Jewish people, the first to hear the word of God, that they may continue to grow in the love of his name and in faithfulness to his covenant.

Almighty and eternal God, long ago you gave your promise to Abraham and his posterity. Listen to your church as we pray that the people you first made your own may arrive at the fullness of redemption.

In July 2007, Pope Benedict once again allowed the use of the Roman Missal, often called the Tridentine Mass. This also meant that the older version of the Good Friday prayer, which asked *'that Almighty God 'would remove the veil from their hearts so that they too may acknowledge Jesus Christ our Lord,'* was now again permissible.

Many Jews and a number of more progressive Roman Catholic thinkers were distressed by this. For example, the request for clarification issued by the Rabbinical Assembly of Conservative Judaism on February 14th expressed surprise at the call for conversion in view of the following points of recent Catholic-Jewish history: (1) Jewish leaders (they said) had succeeded in convincing the Fathers of Vatican II to remove a passage calling for the conversion of the Jews in *Nostra Aetate*; (2) Beginning in 1970 the reformed liturgy (ordinary form) emphasized the spiritual riches of the Jewish people; (3) John Paul II had used the term 'elder brothers' in referring to the Jews; and (4) Cardinal Walter Kasper (head of the Vatican Commission on Religious Relations with the Jews) had announced publicly on several occasions that the Catholic Church no longer maintains an office for the conversion of the Jewish people.

In response to this criticism, Pope Benedict XVI revised the prayer to read:

> *Let us also pray for the Jews: that God our Lord might enlighten their hearts, so that they might know Jesus Christ as the Saviour of all mankind.*
>
> *Almighty and eternal God, whose desire it is that all men might be saved and come to the knowledge of truth, grant in your mercy that as the fullness of mankind enters into your Church, all Israel may be saved, through Christ our Lord. Amen.*

'Clearly Benedict desired here to remove any terms which might still appear to be derogatory ("blindness", "veil", "darkness"),' writes Dr Jeff Mirus, 'and it seems likely that he considered even the term "conversion" to be a red flag, though he left the concept intact. Whatever the case, he retains the spirit of the extraordinary form, with its emphasis not on what the Jewish people already possess, but on what they are lacking, asking that this may be supplied to them through Christ and the Church.' He continues 'Some Jewish representatives are still unhappy. Others understand that any religious body, if it is true to itself, ought to hope and pray that others will receive the spiritual benefits it holds to be so precious. Ultimately, however, the position that the Jews are lacking something is a source of discomfort for those who have come to equate inter-religious progress with a Catholic admission that one religion is as good as another.'

Many Catholics as well as Jews were appalled by this return to a discredited theology. In an attempt to mollify the criticism a revised version was issued in February 2008, but it still included the hope that Jews would eventually recognise Jesus Christ as *'the Saviour of all men.'*

Mary Boys, a Roman Catholic scholar who has worked for a new relationship with the Jews, voiced the dismay of many progressive Roman Catholics. 'I believe that both history and theology offer warrants for respecting the belief and practice of Jews rather than seeking their conversion to Christianity... To seek the conversion of Jews to Christianity is ultimately to seek Judaism's demise. It is fundamental to Christianity that God entered into covenant with the Jewish people – a covenant that, as Pope John Paul II said many times, was "never revoked." God is faithful to covenants, and, therefore the way of Judaism is salvific for Jews. Torah is a path to holiness.'

The Vatican

In December 1993, the Vatican established full diplomatic relations with the modern state of Israel. This happened on the 16th day of the month of Tevet in 5754, three months after the historic White House agreement between Yitzhak Rabin, Prime Minister of Israel, and Yasser Arafat, Chairman of the Palestine Liberation Organisation. For Jews, the Holy See's recognition was more than 'a mere brotherly gesture. It was a powerful symbol of full recognition and legitimacy, an open declaration to the world that Judaism continues to have a place in God's plan for human history. It was a sign that Jews are truly loved by their Catholic brothers and sisters and welcome in the family of nations.'

Christians may only be surprised by such an enthusiastic welcome if they have forgotten that for centuries the Catholic Church saw the banishment of Jews from the Holy Land as a divine punishment for the death of the Son of God. The preamble to the agreement between the Holy See and the State of Israel acknowledged that it had in part been possible because of the 'historic process of reconciliation and growth in mutual understanding and friendship between Catholics and Jews.' To this process CCJ and other member organizations of the International Council of Christians and Jews have made a significant contribution by leading the way in correcting the traditional anti-Judaism of church teaching.

Chapter 9. Wider Links

We need external dialogue of those who live in the same street or in the same village, work in the same factory or study at the same university; We also need internal dialogue, the discussion that goes on in ourselves, in our heads and hearts, whenever we encounter strangers, a person or a book of another religion

Hans Küng

The work of the Council of Christians and Jews has never been confined to Jewish-Christian relations. The CCJ has worked with many religious and interfaith organisations in Britain - too numerous to mention - and played a significant part in the life of the International Council of Christians and Jews.

The Interfaith Network

CCJ was one of the founder members of the Inter Faith Network of the UK (IFN) in 1987 and has given strong support to its work. The Inter Faith Network, as Brian Pearce - at that time its Director - explained to members of CCJ, is unlike CCJ and other interfaith organizations because it has no provision for individual membership and does not have local 'branches.' The Network brings together a wide range of organizations concerned for inter faith relations, which include national representative bodies of faith communities in Britain, as well as national, regional and local inter faith organisations and educational and academic bodies which specialise in inter faith relations and the wider inter faith scene. The Network is for organisations and not individuals. The purpose of the Network is to complement and not to duplicate the work of its member bodies. Brian Pearce also spoke of the increasing interest of the government in encouraging good interfaith relations.

Northern Ireland

CCJ has also used its long experience of inter-religious dialogue to help in Northern Ireland. The CCJ branch in Belfast was one of the few places in Northern Ireland where Catholics and Protestants could not only talk to Jews but also talk to each other. Moreover, CCJ gave considerable help to a cross-community project that reached thousands of young people from both communities. Conferences were held at Armagh and Inniskillen, attended by 160 young people drawn equally from the Catholic and Protestant communities. For several years CCJ staff member, Jonathan Gorsky spoke at a number of school conferences. Gradually an outstanding programme on street violence and prejudice was developed.

Social Cohesion

More recently the growth of terrorism and religious extremism, has led the government to give some support to interfaith work hoping that the religions in Britain could work together for social cohesion. This became even more urgent when it was known that it alienated young men, who had grown up and been educated in Britain, perpetrated the London bombings in 2005.

Relations with Muslims

CCJ has also used the knowledge it has accumulated to contribute to the current search for social cohesion and to addressing the issue of fundamentalism and intolerance and it is often called upon to give advice.

This, of course, has raised the question 'Should CCJ involve itself in dialogue with Muslims?' This has been the subject of repeated discussions at meetings of the CCJ branches, Trustees and Presidents. The decision has always been to concentrate on the bilateral dialogue between Jews and Christians. The CCJ, in Margaret Shepherd's words, 'remained firmly focussed on the bilateral dialogue between Jews and Christians.' This is largely because Christianity has a very special relationship with Judaism. Jews and Christians share some scriptures. There is also still work to be done to heal the legacy of 2,000 years of Christian anti-Judaism. The three way conversations of Jews, Christians and Muslims have a different agenda and dynamic. This is also true of the dialogue of Christians and Muslims, of Jews and Muslims, and of multi-faith dialogue.

Rather sadly, the creation in 1997 of the Three Faiths Forum for dialogue between Jews, Christians and Muslims, was viewed with some suspicion by CCJ. It was thought the new body might compete for support and funding. Friction, reported in some of the religious press, was of no help to either organisation. Today, CCJ and the Three Faiths Forum happily co-operate on a number of projects.

More recently, while maintaining its traditional focus, CCJ has been concerned about the growth of prejudice which has led to increased antisemitism and Islamaphobia. Muslims have been invited to some programmes. CCJ has also expressed its concern about the treatment of asylum seekers.

Other Strategic Partners

There are so many other organisations with which CCJ has arranged joint programmes or to which it has given advice. Space only allows room to give a few examples.

CCJ helped with the newly designed Anne Frank exhibition at Southwark Cathedral. It has co-operated with the Jewish Musical Festival and the Jewish Museum. Both Jewish and Christian bodies approach CCJ for advice on how to contact those with similar interests in the other religion. For instance, Helen Fry and Valerie Norris have attended Russian Orthodox-Jewish meetings in St Petersburg and were able to share with both Russian Christians and Jews information about developments in other parts of the world. CCJ has also brought together Rabbis and pastors of the Black-led churches.

Other strategic partners that should be mentioned include the Board of Deputies of British Jews, Churches Together in Britian and Ireland, the Yad Vashem Institue in Jerusalem, and the Anglo Israel Association. The pages of *Common Ground* show many other links.

There are also many commemorative events at which CCJ is represented. The 900th anniversary of the Crusades – perhaps best forgotten – was marked by an international conference at Emmanuel College, Cambridge on 'Religious Violence with respect to Christians and Jews.' The sixtieth anniversary of the Kinderstransport was also remembered.

International Council of Christians and Jews

CCJ's influence has extended far beyond Britain. Many CCJ members have played an active part in the work of the International Council of Christians and Jews and CCJ directors have usually served on its Executive Committee.

The initiative to create an International Council of Christians and Jews (ICCJ) - established in 1975 - was largely taken by Revd W.W. (Bill) Simpson, who was for many years the indefatigable General Secretary of CCJ. It was fitting, therefore, that some young people from Britain were present in 1990 when a forest grove in Jerusalem was dedicated to the memory of W.W. Simpson.

One of the regular ICCJ Colloquia was held in Southampton, to coincide with the 80th birthday of the pioneering scholar James Parkes. A subsequent Colloquium was again held in Southampton in 1991 and another was held in Manchester in 2012.

The story of the International Council of Christians and Jews has been told in detail by Ruth Weyl. Here there is space only to highlight some of the contributions made to ICCJ by members of the British CCJ.

In 1991, Rabbi Andrew Goldstein of the Northwood and Pinner Liberal Synagogue, presented a paper at a conference held in Hong Kong on the subject of 'The Wisdom traditions in the Bible and Chinese religion'. In 1994, Lord Coggan led an ICCJ delegation to a consultation in Cyprus between Western and Middle Eastern Christians who were concerned for good Jewish-Christian relations.

In 1994 an ICCJ Consultation in Poland concluded with a visit to Treblinka. In the words of Rabbi Julian Jacobs, 'We were all deeply traumatized, we felt more vulnerable than we felt as children. It was from the presence of Polish and other Christian friends that we drew strength and support. And while the thoughts of no two people were exactly alike in a place where the sheer normality of nature seemed both an affront and an expression of hope, it was a binding experience which put new flesh on our discussions.'

In 1995 one of the keynote addresses at the Colloquium in Budapest was given by the Progressive Rabbi Elizabeth Sara. At the same meeting, the former Chief Rabbi Lord Jakobovits introduced a heated debate on moral issues relating to bio-ethics. In the following year, two of the main speakers were from Britain: Lord Coggan and Rabbi Dr Albert Friedlander who both reflected on the verse from Gensis, 3, 9, "Where art thou?' Then in 1998 at the Colloquium in Erlbach, a small place in the former East Germany just across the Czech border, Rabbi Alexandra Wright for London was a speaker.

In 2004, a small consultation between members of the World Council of Churches and the IICJ was held in London, to reflect on how the findings of Jewish-Christian dialogue related to Christian self-understanding. Rabbi Dr Andrew Goldstein, Dr Edward Kessler and Ruth Weyl were members of the ICCJ delegation.

At a preparatory meeting for the Berlin Colloqium in 2009, Rabbi Dr Marc Saperstein, principal of Leo Baeck College in London, gave a paper challenging some accepted views on Jewish-Christian dialogue. He questioned talk about 'the parting of the ways' and suggested instead that there was no sudden rupture and only gradual differentiation. He also said that, although he was a signatory of it, he did not agree with the statement in *Dabru Emet* - the statement on Jewish relations with Christianity drawn up by prominent Jewish scholars in 2000 - that 'without the long history of Christian anti Judaism and Christian violence against the Jews, Nazi ideology could not have taken hold nor could it have been carried out.' Historical records and subsequent examples of genocide - such as in Cambodia - led him to the more pessimistic conclusion that authoritarian government can demonise a minority group with lethal results in a frightening and short period of time without centuries-long tradition of negative attitudes. Rabbi Dr Marc Sapperstein also insisted that no preconditions or ultimatums should be imposed on the partners in dialogue.

The Abrahamic Forum

Several people from Britain have also taken an active part in the Abrahamic Forum which ICCJ established, including Rabbi Dr Charles Middleburgh, Sheikh Zaki Badawi, Rabbi Professor Jonathan Magonet, Dr Martin Forward, who now teaches in the USA, and Dr Amineh Hoti and Sheikh Mumisa from Cambridge. Some British scholars shared in preparing 'The Twelve Points of Berlin,' which summarise the progress made in Jewish Christian Dialogue.

ICCJ Young Leaders programme

Several people from Britain have been deeply influenced by their participation in the ICCJ Young Leaders programme. Canon Andrew White, now Vicar in Baghdad, is perhaps the best known. In 2007 the ICCJ Young leaders met in Britain in a village near Northampton.

Although not part of ICCJ's programmes mention should again be made of the participation of some ICCJ members in the very important Roman Catholic-Jewish dialogue meeting held in London in 2000 and the series of scholarly conferences on 'The Holocaust in an Age of Genocide, arranged by Dr Elizabeth Maxwell.

More could be said of the work of members of CCJ in schools and colleges and in wider interfaith dialogue; but this is enough to be a reminder that the influence of CCJ stretches far beyond programmes specifically organised by CCJ.

Section Two: The People

Chapter 10. Local Branches: More about People than Theology.

'To make something real, you must make it local'

'Dialogue begins when people meet each other' is the first of the four Principles of Dialogue. As vital as is the work of education in informing people about another faith and in removing ignorance and prejudice, there is no substitute for meeting members of that faith and getting to know them personally. It helps to know what it means to live as a Christian or as a Jew. This is why from the very beginning CCJ has put great emphasis on building up a network of local branches.

For 70 years, branches of the Council of Christians and Jews in the UK have provided Jews and Christians with the opportunity to meet, build relationships and become friends. 'What makes dialogue possible is our common humanity, created in the image of God. We all experience the joys and sorrows of human life, we are citizens of one country, we face the same problems, we all live in God's presence.'

The value of meeting, of what the one-time Methodist leader, Pauline Webb called the 'dialogue of the cup of tea' cannot be over-estimated. Often when people return from a conference, they talk about the people they have met and the friendships they have made, but when asked what the speakers said, they may find it hard to remember!

But the establishment of friendships take time. Past hurt and prejudice has to be laid aside. It is fundamental to establish trust and the confidence that the other has no ulterior missionary or political agenda. There will be ignorance to dispel.

Currently there are some 36 CCJ branches. A glance at state of the art CCJ website (http://www.ccj.org.uk) gives up to date information about their varied and lively programmes. The branches of the Council of Christians and Jews represent Jewish-Christian relations at community level. CCJ is proud of the work its branches do in promoting understanding between Jews and Christians in all walks of life.

Brighton, Cardiff, Leeds, Oxford and Newcastle and several branches in London, were established in the 1940s, soon after the national CCJ was formed.

In 1993 Cardiff and Redbridge CCJs celebrated their 50th anniversaries. Cardiff held a dinner at the International Hotel. Speakers included Lord Tonypandy, Rabbi Dr Norman Solomon and Rabbi Elaina Rothman. Redbridge arranged a cultural exchange and celebration, 'a wonderful evening of speech, music, food, and good fellowship,' attended by over 200 people. In the same year the Hampstead Branch, which was founded in 1947 but sadly and worryingly for this area with a very significant Jewish population had become dormant, was happily re-launched at a meeting attended by over 100 people. The main speaker was Bishop Richard Harries, newly elected as chair of CCJ, who had been a curate at Hampstead Parish Church. Hull's turn to celebrate its Jubilee came in 1997 when 'fifty years of co-operation, inspiration and information - and not a little fun – came together in an almost magical way at the Pryme Street Synagogue.'

Each decade has seen new branches set up or older ones revived. As demographics change this is and always will be an on-going challenge for the CCJ. The Northern Ireland CCJ was formed in 1996 when the inaugural address was given by Lord Coggan.

In some parts of the country the Jewish population is significant, in other places Jews are heavily outnumbered by Christians. In both religions there are different traditions, so perhaps the first time a Baptist meets a member of the Orthodox Churches, or a member of an Orthodox synagogue meets a member of a Liberal synagogue, may be at a CCJ meeting.

There is not space to give a history of the local branches. Instead, an attempt may be made to build a montage of some branch activities that hopefully will bring back good memories for some readers and make others realise what they are missing!

Because there are so many facets to a religion, there is much to learn, much to discuss, music and art to appreciate, and festivals to enjoy together.

Festivals

Meetings quite often relate to festivals. In 1990, the Redbridge Branch and the North London branch arranged demonstration Seders and Manchester a 'Purim Social Evening.' In 1991, Birmingham arranged a Sukkot social evening. In 1993, North London CCJ had an evening comparing Hanukkah and Advent. In 1998, it was Hull's turn to hold a Purim evening at which 'laughter prevailed.'

The Seder understandably is of particular interest to Christians, because Jesus' Last Supper may have been a Passover meal, yet many Christians do not understand its role in Jewish life and Judaism. After an unfortunate raising of tensions between the leaderships of the Methodist Church and Jewish communities in 2010, the CCJ and its partners held a Demonstration Seder at the 2011 Methodist Conference. Over one third of all delegates to the conference attended. The Festivals and their rituals can become conduits not only for understanding but also healing.

Food

On many occasions the sharing of food brings people together. Food – usually with samples – also has been the subject of several meetings. In St Albans in 2000, the branch had a talk about Jewish and Middle Eastern foods by the famous TV cook and writer, Claudia Roden. People were - and always are - amazed to learn that fish and chips were introduced by Jewish and Irish immigrants. Finchley also had a talk in 2002 on Jewish Food. In the same year Tanya Joyce wrote in *Common Ground* about 'The Leaven in the Loaf.' Staines in 2004 had two talks on Food (with samples of course!) – one on Jewish Festival Food and the other on Christian Festival Food. Soon afterwards members were invited by the Branch Chairman Fr William Whittaker to ring the Bells St Mary's, Stanwell, to help them lose weight!

Music

Where words divide, music often unites - as evidenced by the variety of choral events that are arranged across the country by the CCJ groups. In 1991, Radlett CCJ arranged a programme of 'Music across the Faiths.' Avon CCJ also arranged an evening entitled 'Make a Joyful Noise to the Lord.' At this, choirs from St Michael's Church on the Mount, the Bristol and West Progressive Jewish Congregation and the local Roman Catholic Church all took part. In 1996, Brighton CCJ arranged an evening of psalms, chants and anthems sung by the choirs of the New Synagogue and St Peter's Church. In the following year, the choir of the Progressive Synagogue and of the Church of the Sacred Heart arranged a choral evening. Staines Jewish Community to mark its Diamond Anniversary invited members of the Jewish Male Choir to sing at the Civic Service, at which the Chief Rabbi Dr Jonathan Sacks was the speaker.

When in 2003, thanks to the hard work of Canon Jim Richardson, Bournemouth CCJ was re-launched, music was part of the event. At the opening meeting, attended by over 100 people, the theme was 'The Psalms in Jewish and Christian traditions.' A subsequent meeting was on 'The Impact of Religious Art in Jewish and Christian traditions.' Enfield in 2004 held a joint choral celebration of Christmas and Chanukah with a children's choir from St Monica's school and from Palmers Green and Southgate Synagogue. Redbridge CCJ backed a local project to encourage awareness that the arts can lead to a deeper experience of spirituality.

CCJ Lincoln in its annual Chanukah and Advent Festival of Light at Lincoln Cathedral always has a choir of Jews and Christians as well as local Church of England primary school choirs. The Jewish choir of *Oxford-Shir* are regular contributors to CCJ Oxford's hugely varied annual programme.

Visits

Visits to Synagogues always arouse great interest, especially when the Torah scrolls are displayed. The long history of many churches and their architectural interest is also fascinating. Outings are also popular and the shared experiences deepen friendships. In 1993 Redbridge CCJ visited the old synagogue in Chatham and then attended evensong at Rochester Cathedral. In the following year they went to Lincoln.

In 2005 members of Hull CCJ visited Beth Shalom (the House of Peace), which is a Holocaust Museum near Newark in Nottinghamshire. In May 2000 members of Leeds CCJ took part in a walking tour of Jewish York, including Clifford's Tower, where the Jews of York were martyred in 1189. In 2001, Southend branch members were invited to the Houses of Parliament for a tour and dinner by David Amess, MP for Southend West. The following year members of the North London branch visited the AJEX Museum on Holocaust Memorial Day. In the same year Kent CCJ were entertained by the Archbishop, George Carey, at his Palace at Canterbury. In 2003 Hendon and

Golders Green paid a visit to the National Gallery. In 2007 Hillingdon's Annual Guided Coach Tour was to the British Library and St Paul's Cathedral.

These are not visits just for the sake of a day out, nor only for education, but proactive opportunities for one-to-one dialogue.

Learning about Each Other

Many of the talks given at meetings introduce people to the history or art or literature of one or other religion. This is also often a chance to learn more about one's own religion. Examples of this abound. For example, in Edinburgh in 1991 the then Moderator of the General Assembly of the Church of Scotland, Dr W B R Macmillan, spoke about 'Covenant and Service,' which are two key words to the Jew and the Christian. In the same year Professor David Daiches spoke about 'Translating the Hebrew Bible.'

The intellectual question of the relationship of Jews and Christians - its past and its future - has naturally been a central part of programmes and a key interest of the CCJ members. Not all can afford or have the time to study for a degree or to go to the Parkes Institute at Southampton and other centres of learning. The CCJ branches act as regional evening classes providing intellectual stimulation, contemporary scholarship and space to discuss. Certainly the spectrum of perspectives branches offer is wide. Examples are the late Archbishop Worlock's Southport class on the importance of positive co-operation between Jews and Christians, including the fostering of world peace and mutual education; or the Bristol CCJ lecture series by Dr

Gavin D'Costa and Rabbi Hugo Gryn. Another example is Professor Martin Goodman's talk at Hull CCJ on the question, 'What changed the Romans' amused toleration of their Jewish subjects into an orgy of destruction in the first and second centuries of the Common Era?' In his answer he referred to the cost to the Romans of the capture and destruction of Jerusalem in 66 C.E. and the subsequent siege of Massada. 'The marginalisation of the Jews occurred at the same time as the birth of the Church, and did not precede it.'

There is also the constant urge to break new ground, as with Rabbi Clive Lawton's address to the Hillingdon CCJ. He reaffirmed the importance of dialogue, but meaningful dialogue should not avoid contentious subjects, but should include 'eye to eye' contact and robust argument.

Yet dialogue should never be too serious: religious people must laugh at themselves, like the CCJ Edinburgh group who were educated in 'Jewish Humour' by Arnold Rabinowitz. There was no doubt a lot of humour when over 300 people turned up at Christ Church, Bath to hear Rabbi Lionel Blue.

Israel

From its early days the subject of the State of Israel and its relation to Palestine and the Palestinians has been a topic that is never very far from the CCJ agenda. Important names in the Christian and Jewish communities have often spoken to CCJ on this subject - for example, Stuart Randall, MP, at Hull CCJ; Mrs June Jacobs, then Chair of the Foreign Affairs Committee of the Board of Deputies to

Enfield CCJ; Edinburgh CCJ had a talk from Dr Ezra Golombok, Director of the Israel Information Centre in Scotland.

The Holocaust

Remembrance of the Shoah is bound to be a central part of CCJ's work, as is clear from the activities of many branches such as Glasgow CCJ's 1991 exhibition on the Holocaust, entitled 'Remembering for the Future.' Merseyside CCJ in partnership with Liverpool's cathedrals has staged exhibitions including art, word and images. On one such occasion, Naomi Lopian spoke for the first time about her father who was a survivor of the death camps and she also read from his book *Die Lange Nacht*.

Holocaust Remembrance Day and Yom Ha Shoah are occasions when Christians join Jews in remembrance and in the shared determination that such mass murder will never be repeated. Many synagogues, some churches and some branches arrange such times of remembrance. CCJ Oxford's staging the Yom HaShoah commemoration with the Oxford Jewish community and including all the Christian Church leaders of the City is one such example.

History is made and seminal moments come into people's lives through many CCJ branch events. Who could ever forget the heart-rendingly moving talk to CCJ Hillingdon on 'Memories of the Holocaust' by Revd Leslie Hardman, one of the first Jewish chaplains to enter Belsen, when it was liberated. He told of some 60 German guards who were still in the camp at liberation, but who were not attacked. One survivor, whose parents had been killed, had the opportunity to kill the guards, 'but my Jewish conscience wouldn't allow me to kill them.'

Christians in remembering the Holocaust dare not forget that their past prejudice has contributed so much to the suffering of the Jewish people. For example it was in Norwich that the first blood libel occurred in 1144. This tragic event was recalled with deep regret when Norwich Branch, to mark CCJ's 60th Anniversary, arranged a concert in Norwich Cathedral where psalms and songs were sung by the cathedral choir, the Zemel Choir and St John's Wood Liberal Choir.

Any Questions

As with the popular BBC Radio 4 series "Any Questions?" panels are popular. CCJ Brighton and Hove would annually organise a panel with the Mayor, rabbis, academics and clerics.

CCJ Oxford arranged for the Board of Deputies' 'Jewish Way of Life Exhibition' to be held at the iconic Dorchester Abbey in Oxfordshire in 2010. Working with the Rector, Canon Sue Booys, CCJ staged a number of events around the exhibition which include their own Any Questions. The panel comprised Rt Revd Colin Fletcher, Bishop of Dorchester, Mohammed Amin a former partner of Global Accountancy firm PWC, Hon Barney Leith, of the Baha'i faith and Rabbi Dr Jonathan Romain. It took the BBC Radio Oxford presenter Phil Mercer to keep them in order!

Outreach

CCJ Branches are not just inward looking groups for mutual enrichment. Many branches take seriously the task of educating the wider public and being on the look-out for signs of prejudice, racism and antisemitism.

For many years, Manchester CCJ has arranged a 'Friendship Week,' which, besides talks and social evenings, includes invitations to services in a synagogue or a church.

Local branches have also been active in arranging programmes for schools and in supplying speakers to churches, synagogues and other organisations. Hull CCJ presented sets of books on Judaism and Jewish-Christian relationships to some of the city's senior schools. Leeds CCJ has a long record of proactive work with schools. They have recently established an annual trip for local fifth and sixth formers to visit the Beth Shalom Holocaust Memorial Museum in Nottingham. Each branch brings a creativity of its own to its locality, like Eastbourne's schools poster competition and poetry competition. Students were asked to write a poem on 'Please Understand Me' as though they were themselves suffering by being 'different' in some way.

CCJ must be ever vigilant in defending its right and proper function to promote harmonious Christian-Jewish relations. A member of Southend CCJ, on a visit to a local park for an evangelistic event called 'Praise in the Park,' noticed one of the stalls had a display of anti-Israel propaganda. After protests to the organisers, CCJ eventually received an apology.

Being proactive members of the community is part of being

a CCJ member. It is common for CCJ members to write to the local press or local radio if they read or hear remarks which are antisemitic or anti-Israel.

Social Concerns

Jews and Christians share many concerns for justice and human rights. It took the speaker at Wimbledon CCJ, Mr Paul Riddell, from the Commission for Racial Equality, in 1997, the European Year against Racism, to remind CCJ nationally that the CCJ was constitutionally committed 'to fighting the evils of prejudice, intolerance and discrimination.' In 1998, members of the North-East branch of CCJ took an active part in a high-profile conference on 'Social and Spiritual Regeneration,' at which Cardinal Basil Hume was one of the speakers. The Provost and Branch Chairman, the Very Revd Nicholas Coulton, long time CCJ member, chaired the final session.

CCJ in Glasgow caused its membership to sit up when they arranged an interesting evening on 'Setting Down Roots in Scotland', with a talk by Mr Sassoon Judah, who had been brought up in a religiously observant Jewish family in Bombay. When his mother went to buy food, because of her colour she was redirected to the nearby Hallal butcher. Derek Goh, who was born to Buddhist parents in Malaysia, also talked about his experiences.

The Annual Conference

An important date in CCJ's year is the Annual Conference. For many years this was held at Hengrave Hall near Bury St Edmunds, but more recently was held at the Ammerdown Retreat and Conference Centre at Radstock, near Bath.

Hengrave Hall was a grand Tudor house near Bury St Edmunds, which, at the time was run by an ecumenical community. Already in 1990 the Conference was about the Environment. At several other conferences the subject has been what Jews and Christians can contribute to a more healthy society.

Ammerdown is an ecumenical community of which, for many years, Sisters of Sion were members. The 2001 Ammerdown Conference led by Sister Margaret Shepherd and Jonathan Gorsky, with a record attendance of fifty-five people, is a good example. The focus was on 'community'. This involved looking at the Jesus community in rural Galilee compared to the Mediterranean cities in which St Paul was at home as well as comparing them with modern communities, including Iona, Taize and L'Arche. The week was followed by a weekend on 'Images of Jesus – how Jesus has been seen by writers and artists through the centuries.' 'Every day started with a talk, group work, lunch and a free afternoon spent leisurely in the Ammerdown gardens...There was a second talk later in the afternoon and a video in the evening. The programme integrated Biblical study with contemporary concerns; each evening was given over to music, prayer and living experience of a different community.' No description of the programme, however, can give a sense of the personal enrichment to Jewish and Christian participants in sharing life together for several days.

The 2003, Ammerdown Study Week concentrated on the 'Songs of the Servant passages in Isaiah, which have been a source of much controversy between Jews and Christians. 'That we were able to spend a day together on precisely these chapters,' said Sister Margaret Shepherd, 'shows how far we have progressed in the last sixty years.'

In recent years the pattern and choice of venues has been more varied. In October 2009, a special Branches' Conference was held at Wycliffe Centre, High Wycombe. Speakers included the well- known Rabbi Dr Norman Solomon and Michael Wakelin, a former Head of Religion and Ethics at the BBC. Delegates also had the chance to question two Vice Presidents of CCJ, Baroness Richardson and Dr Lionel Kopelowitz as well as CCJ President Rabbi Jonathan Wittenberg. They discussed the financing of branches with Mark Herbert of the Unity Trust Bank. On the Wednesday afternoon Maurice Ostro, Vice Chairman, outlined his hopes for the future of CCJ. CCJ member and doctoral researcher, Wendy Fiddler's address on 'Anglican Attitudes towards Jews in England in 2009' based on her own research provoked deep discussion.

The experience of seeing and hearing is a hallmark of much CCJ work. Indeed its current project Encounters3 works with rabbis, and Christian clergy and community faith leaders. Experiential seminars and visits are the substance of this project led by Fiona Hulbert, such as the day for Christian leaders looking at Rites of Passage held at a synagogue in London. This included the chance of observe a Bar Mitzvah as guests of the family.

Linking the Branches

Over the years there have been regular meetings for representatives of the branches, thanks in large measure to the energy and enthusiasm of Mrs Rose Owen, as chair of the Association of Local Branches. On her retirement in 1993 she was thanked by the Bishop of Oxford for her 'sterling work.'

In 2009 the 'C4C Communities for Change' project was launched with the aim of restructuring amd reinvigorating the work of the branches. As mentioned above, in October 2009, a special branches' conference was held at the Wycliffe Centre, High Wycombe.

Delegates went home from this successful event with a renewed confidence, which was shown during the first national Interfaith Week in November 2010. CCJ arranged more events, up and down the country, than any other interfaith organisation. CCJ's contribution to this national initiative was as diverse as it was comprehensive. In Staines, Rabbi Jonathan Romain spoke on 'Interfaith Dialogue: Love-in or Religious Punch Up.' In Guildford, Simon Keyes of St Ethelburga's Centre for Reconciliation and Peace in London led a discussion on 'The Power of Apology.' In Newcastle and Harlow, CCJ held 'Open House' evenings to introduce guests to the Synagogue.

The electronic newsletter 'Bridging Branches' now links branches and will continue to encourage and stimulate them.

Chapter 11. At the Centre (1): Outstanding Leaders

If a person's gift is leadership, let him do so with diligence
St Paul

CCJ is about people – people meeting, learning about each other's religious beliefs and practices, becoming friends and working together for a society shaped by the moral values shared by the Jewish and Christian faiths. So who are the 'people'? Many are known, respected and loved in their local branches. Other dedicated people have had a leadership role in CCJ as a national organization. They, naturally, figure prominently at prestigious public events. None of the leading figures, however, have been mere figureheads, but all have taken a real and informed interest in the work of CCJ, which has benefited by their wisdom and wide experience.

Patron

From its early days CCJ has been blessed by the Patronage of Her Majesty the Queen. She has shown real interest in its work and hosted a number of receptions.

In 1994 CCJ was honoured by a Royal Reception at St James' Palace, as well as by a reception at 10 Downing Street. CCJ's Diamond Jubilee was celebrated in style with many special events. The highlight was again a Royal Reception at St James's Palace hosted by her Majesty the

Queen and the Duke of Edinburgh. There was also a further Reception at 10 Downing Street, at which the Prime Minister, Rt Hon Tony Blair, made an unexpected appearance and at which his wife Cherie Blair QC stressed the continuing importance of CCJ. To mark CCJ's 70th anniversary, a private reception was held at Crosby Hall on the banks of the Thames, by Mr Christopher Moran. The Queen and HRH the Duke of Edinburgh were the Guests of Honour.

Joint-Presidents

Christian and Jewish leaders, as Joint Presidents, have given and continue to give strong support. Archbishop Robert Runcie, who had often spoken on Jewish-Christian issues, retired in 1990. During his time the Joint Presidents met for the first time for an afternoon's private discussion. These meetings have now become an annual event.

Robert Runcie's successor Archbishop George Carey was an equally strong supporter of CCJ. George Carey's concern for better relations with Jews started, he says, through his reading as a young person of the suffering of the Jewish people in the Holocaust. 'I was outraged,' he writes, 'by the pitiless way they were treated for the most contemptible of reasons. As a young Christian I was also concerned as I began to see that Christianity was implicated in it, because of the way its theology was twisted to accuse the Jews of causing the death of Jesus Christ. When I was on the staff of Oakhill Theological College - a college in the evangelical tradition - I started to attend CCJ meetings in the Southgate area and met a Rabbi for the first time! I found him to be an immensely interesting man and, what amazed me greatly, was that we saw eye to eye on a number of theological issues.'

At Oakhill, I also taught a class on the New Testament and I found myself more and more convinced that the roots of antisemitism are to be found in the New Testament itself. This was a great shock. The roots are there in the Gospels - particularly John's gospel. To be sure, the story is also about Jews persecuting Christians - the death of Stephen, for example - but the later church found ammunition in the gospels to feed antisemitism.'

Archbishop Rowan Williams has been deeply committed to strengthening the bonds with the Jewish community and untiring in his support of CCJ. On his appointment Chief Rabbi Jonathan Sacks said: 'Rowan Williams is a quite exceptional thinker and man of God, and I look forward to the same warm friendship that I had with his predecessor, which did so much to improve Jewish-Christian relationships.' He and Jonathan Sacks have attended a number of events together and they have been on joint visits both to Auschwitz and to Israel and the Palestinian Territories.

Besides often speaking on the subject and attending events, which bring Jews and Christians together, Rowan Williams has made a point of releasing a special message for each Holocaust Memorial Day and of sending his greetings to the Jewish community at Rosh Hashanah, which marks the start of the Jewish New Year. The message for Rosh Hashanah 2007 is one example:

> 'I am writing at this beginning of a new year for Jewish communities in this country and around the world, to

offer you my warmest wishes for a good year ahead and for one in which our personal and community relationships will be further strengthened and deepened.

The festival of Rosh Hashanah and the solemnities of the High Holy Days through to the Day of Atonement, which follow, have a strong resonance for Christian communities who share the same scriptural heritage. During these days Jewish families and communities will come together, as they have done for millennia, to pray and to renew a profound commitment to the foundational values of the life of faith in God. The renewal, year by year, of this grateful commitment to God's calling and covenant is the wellspring of that intense vision of justice, mercy and mutual respect that is so central a dimension of the many gifts Judaism has given to the world.

I sincerely hope that all that may have marred the year past - a rising level of antisemitic incidents and the anxieties and insecurities arising from conflict in the Middle East - will be alleviated in the coming year. I particularly hope and pray for the return of Gilad Shalit, Ehud Goldwasser and Eldad Regev to their families.

May the year ahead indeed be one, which includes sweetness in our relations and for our country.

The Moderators of the Church of Scotland, who only hold office for one year, have also been Joint Presidents. Distance has made it difficult for some of them to be much involved at a UK level, but all have backed CCJ's work in Scotland, where there have been lively branches in

Edinburgh and Glasgow. Unfortunately the dwindling Jewish community in Edinburgh has necessitated the closure of that particular branch but the Glasgow one continues to be as vibrant as ever.

The Heads of the Roman Catholic Church have all been active Joint Presidents. Cardinal Hume, who died in 1999, was keen to be seen as a friend to the Jewish community (and was indeed a personal friend of successive Chief Rabbis). He spoke sincerely and profoundly about the experience of visiting the concentration camp at Auschwitz in Poland. Cardinal Hume was succeeded by Cormac Murphy-O'Connor, who was installed as the tenth Archbishop of Westminster on 22 March 2000 and who was created Cardinal by Pope John Paul II in February 2001. On his retirement, Archbishop Vincent Nichols was installed as the eleventh Archbishop of Westminster on 21 May 2009. North of the border, Cardinal Keith Patrick O'Brien, Archbishop of St Andrews and Edinburgh, Cardinal Thomas Joseph Winning Archbishop of Glasgow until 2001 and his successor Archbishop Mario Joseph Conti have given their support to CCJ Scotland

The Free Churches' Moderator, who normally holds office for five years, is also a Joint-President of CCJ. Theirs is not an easy task for they represent a wide spectrum of theological opinions and perspective on Jewish – Christian dialogue, to say nothing of the passionate and diverse views held by many in the Free Churches on the Israel–Palestine conflict. The leader of the Greek Orthodox Church in the UK, The Archbishop of Thyateira and Great Britain, is also a Joint-President and keen supporter of CCJ.

Lord Sacks has been Chief Rabbi and a Joint-President

throughout the twenty years covered in this book. He has been untiring in his support for CCJ. He dedicated his book *Faith in the Future* 'to the members of the Council of Christians and Jews.' Jonathan Sacks described his meeting with Pope Benedict XVI during his visit to Britain in 2010 as 'an epiphany'. 'Soul touched soul across the boundaries of faith, and there was a blessed moment of healing'

For more than fifty years the Chief Rabbi was the sole Jewish President and was seen by many Christians as representing the whole Jewish community, although Progressive Jews wanted their own Joint President. In 1998, after much discussion, Rabbi Dr Albert Friedlander was appointed as an Associate President and subsequently became a Joint-President. Dr Albert Friedlander, who was Rabbi of Westminster Synagogue and a distinguished scholar, particularly on issues relating to the Holocaust, was highly regarded both in the Jewish and the wider community.

Albert Friedlander was succeeded by Rabbi Dr Tony Bayfield, - a former Head of the Movement for Reform Judaism - who has for many years been a leading figure in Christian-Jewish dialogue, especially as a co-convenor of the Manor House Group and as an author.

More recently, the number of Jewish Presidents has further increased to include Rabbi Danny Rich, Chief Executive of Liberal Judaism; Rabbi Jonathan Wittenberg, Senior Rabbi of the Assembly of Masorti Synagogues; and Rabbi Dr Abraham Levy, Spiritual Head of Spanish and Portuguese Jews' Congregation.

Vice-Presidents

There is also a distinguished list of Vice-Presidents: Lord Carey of Clifton, former Archbishop of Canterbury from 1991 to 2002; Revd Dr David Coffey, President of the Baptist World Alliance; Mrs Elizabeth Corob, Co-founder of the Sidney and Elizabeth Corob Charitable Trust, whose husband Sidney Corob served for many years as Vice-Chairman; Henry Grunwald QC, former President of the Board of Deputies of British Jews; Lord Harries of Pentregarth, former Bishop of Oxford and former Chairman of CCJ; Rt Rev Dr Christopher Herbert, former Bishop of St. Albans and former Chairman of CCJ; Dr Lionel Kopelowitz, a retired General Practitioner and former President of the Board of Deputies of British Jews; Sir Michael Latham, a former Conservative MP and former Trustee of CCJ; Clive Marks FCA, a former Treasurer and Trustee of CCJ; Cardinal Cormac Murphy-O'Connor, former Archbishop of Westminster; The Hon Gerard Noel FRSL, an author and fellow of the Royal Society of Literature; Revd. Baroness Richardson of Calow, the first woman President of the Methodist Conference (1992-1993) and a cross-bench member of the House of Lords; R Stephen Rubin, chairman of the Pentland Group; and Sir Timothy Sainsbury, a politician and leading business-man.

The Executive Committee and Board of Trustees.

The governing body, which has been variously called 'The Executive Committee,' 'The Board' or 'The Trustees' usually meets four times a year.

Chairmen

The various chairmen during this period, although people with many responsibilities, have given much time and good leadership to CCJ. Dr Edward Carpenter, a distinguished former Dean of Westminster Abbey, was chairman of the CCJ Executive from 1987 until 1992. For a year, Lord Coggan, former Archbishop of Canterbury, who had been Edward Carpenter's predecessor in the chair, returned as a very energetic Acting Chairman.

Richard Harries

In 1993 Lord Coggan handed the reins to Richard Harries, then Bishop of Oxford, for whom improving Christian-Jewish relations was already a high priority. As a child towards the end of World War II, Richard was taken to the cinema, but as the Pathé news was shown, he was told to keep his eyes shut, but, of course, he did have a peek and glimpsed the emaciated figures of prisoners in Belsen being released. At school he witnessed distasteful and unpleasant scenes of a boy being taunted with shouts of 'Jew boy.' Then at Cuddesdon Theological College, Richard heard a talk by James Parkes, the great Anglican pioneer and possibly the intellectual founder of the CCJ who showed the Churches' deep responsibility for antisemitism. He also spent one term in East Jerusalem, when it was still under the control of Jordan.

Richard Harries was an active member of the Manor House group, which was an informal dialogue group of rabbis and clergy who met for several years and produced the book *Dialogue with a Difference*. It was largely through Richard's efforts that the 1988 Lambeth Conference of Anglican bishops commended the important document 'Jews, Christians and Muslims: the Way of Dialogue.' This was the first time that the Anglican Communion had addressed the subject. Although the original draft, which referred only to Jews, was watered down, the document was of great significance. It recognised that Judaism is a living religion and affirmed the special bond between Judaism and Christianity. As chairman of CCJ, Richard Harries continued to press for a new Christian appreciation of Judaism – seen for example in his book *After the Evil.* He also argued, as we have seen, that Christians should not try to convert Jews. Richard also convened the scholarly Jewish-Christian-Muslim group in Oxford which, to share the fruits of their deliberations, produced the book *Abraham's Children.*

Christopher Herbert

Richard's successor was Christopher Herbert who was at the time Bishop of St Alban's. Bishop Herbert, who was ordained in 1967, had been Vicar of the Bourne, near Farnham, a Director of Ordinands and Canon of Guildford Cathedral. He became Archdeacon of Dorking in 1990 and Bishop of St Alban's in 1995. Besides his many diocesan responsibilities, Christopher Herbert devoted much time to CCJ. He was also a member of a House of Lords' select committee that considered a private member's bill about euthanasia and assisted suicide.

Nigel McCulloch

Bishop Christopher Herbert retired as Chairman of CCJ in 2006. His place was taken by Nigel McCulloch, who had been Bishop of Taunton and then Bishop of Wakefield before moving to Manchester, where he quickly established good relations with the large Jewish community in the city. Nigel McCulloch has been described as 'one of the most experienced bishops in the Church of England.' He is the author of several books, a former columnist for *The Times*, and a frequent broadcaster.

After his first year in office as Chairman, Bishop McCulloch shared his reflections. In particular, he highlighted the Board's own commitment to the purposes of CCJ as defined in the constitution and emphasised the bilateral focus of CCJ and its social rather than theological interests. He pointed out that the permissive nature of clause 2.2 did enable discussions with Muslims and about Islam, although the Constitution did not allow their full inclusion as a third equal partner. Under his leadership the organizational structure of CCJ has been streamlined.

Vice Chairmen

Sadly three of the Vice-Chairmen in the past twenty years, Bishop Gerald Mahon, Bishop Charles Henderson and Sidney Corob have died. Tributes are paid to them in the subsequent chapter entitled 'The Souls of the Righteous.' Bishop Henderson's place was taken by Bishop Bernard Longley. The Vice-Chairmen, at the time of writing, are Christopher Morran and Maurice Ostro. Christopher Morran is a successful entrepreneur and well-known businessman. He also has a strong commitment to wider society, supporting institutions in national heritage, arts, health and wellbeing, faith and international relations.

In a recent article Christopher Morran spoke of the new and

additional challenges that modern-day faith communities and society at large face today, which would perplex and dismay those who founded the CCJ.

> 'Faith,' he said 'matters not just for individuals, but for communities and society. Faith has helped shape almost every aspect of our national and private lives – schools, hospitals and orphanages are all manifestations of that faith. Faith, therefore, is not ephemeral and abstract; it is the solid theoretical foundation upon which practical action is built. If faith is allowed to rot, then the actions which flow from it will similarly decay. Such has been the advance of aggressive secularism that I am increasingly concerned that the decline of faith in God is unpicking many of the strands which bind our communities together and which bring depth and meaning to our being'

Maurice Ostro is Chief Executive of the Fayre Share Foundation and has won the 'Outstanding Contribution to Business Award.' He is also an active supporter of a wide range of Jewish charities. In 2011, working with the Faiths Forum for London, he organised a meeting of Faith leaders and representatives of religious groups in London to look at how they might mobilise their communities and unlock civic potential in the capital. The day-long event at King's College was hosted by the Mayor of London Boris Johnson, who said: 'London's faith communities are a huge reservoir of goodwill and commitment with a vital role to play in helping young people to stay away from crime, realise their aspirations and achieve their potential. They offer support to the elderly and other vulnerable groups, as well as engendering community spirit, from volunteering and mentoring to philanthropic giving. These are issues that Londoners care about, so let's harness this impulse for good, which will bring massive benefits for future generations in our city.'

Honorary Officers

Rabbi Dr Harry Levy and Revd Eric Allen, long-serving Honorary Secretaries were both in office at the start of the nineties. In 1992, after many years devoted work, Harry Levy decided it was time to retire. His place was taken by Hayim Pinner, then recently retired as Secretary of the Board of Deputies of British Jews, in which position he had been unfailing in his support for CCJ. After his premature death, his place was taken by Mrs Rosalind Preston, who has held a number of important positions in the voluntary sector, and served with great distinction as a Joint Honorary Secretary from 1997-2005.

Harry Levy

Dr Harry Levy was born and brought up in Paddington, West London, and was educated at University College London, and at a leading Talmudical academy, the Yeshiva Etz Chaim, in the East End. He also studied at Jews' College, the main training ground for the ministry, where he later became a lecturer.

Before the Second World War he served synagogues at Bayswater and Hampstead Garden Suburb. After the war, he was Rabbi of Hampstead Synagogue. In the war, he was a chaplain to forces in both the Middle East (where he was captured by the Afrika Corps, but managed to escape) and the British Army of the Rhine. In the latter capacity, he was among the British troops who liberated Bergen-Belsen.

The memory of the days at Bergen-Belsen never left him. Suddenly, Harry Levy was faced with the problems of dying inmates in one of the most obscene death camps. He supervised the burial of inmates who had died before his eyes, and conducted services for those who were able to take part. He always spoke movingly of the incredulous reaction of prisoners who, for the first time in their lives, saw an army officer, wearing not Nazi insignia but a Star of David badge on his cap. He wrote a book about his experiences, *Witness To Evil: Belsen*. Harry Levy was a prolific author. People often read early editions of *Common Ground* just to learn from his many book reviews.

Eric Allen

Revd Eric Allen who served as Honorary Secretary with unfailing courtesy and faithfulness from 1986-2006, has been a leading member of the United Reformed Church. As so often, it was personal experience that first motivated Eric's lifelong commitment to Christian-Jewish friendship. As a teenager he got to know some of the Kindertransport children who were temporarily cared for by Quaker families in St Albans in 1939-40. The next year some Jewish boys joined his class at school. His church also gave hospitality to an Austrian Jew, Mrs Kahane, whose husband was caught fleeing through Holland and then murdered. In 1950, during the Christmas Vacation, Eric who was by then studying at the Congregational Church's New College, London, visited Mrs Kahane in St Alban's. A fellow student, Pastor H Schreiber, who had served in the German army, came with him. 'Before we left he personally apologised to her for the Holocaust ... it was a traumatic and tearful moment and marked for me a desire to learn about the Barmen Declaration and the newly published writings of Dietrich Bonhoeffer.'

Throughout his ministry Eric worked closely with neighbouring Jewish communities and has been actively involved in many dialogue groups, as well supporting the Centre for Judaism and Jewish Christian Relations, headed by Rabbi Norman Solomon, at the Selly Oak Colleges in Birmingham.

Following Eric's retirement, Revd Jonathan Dean, a minister of the United Reformed Church of St Andrews in Hampstead, was welcomed as Honorary Secretary. Jonathan was also adviser on Jewish affairs to the United Reformed Church.

Honorary Treasurers

Sir Sigmund Sternberg, who has given so much of his life to promoting interfaith dialogue and had been Honorary Treasurer of CCJ for many years, resigned in 1993. Lord Finsberg, who had been Conservative MP for Hampstead and Highgate, took his place and subsequently in 1995 became Joint Honorary Treasurer. His sudden death in 1996 was a shock to his many friends. The Christian Honorary Treasurer for a time was Mr A Prendegarst, who was a former Lord Mayor of Westminster and later a High Sheriff of London. He was soon succeeded by Michael Latham who served until the end of 1999.

The responsibilities of the Honorary Officers are now shared by the Trustees, who, besides the Chairman and Vice-Chairmen include Sir Sydney Chapman, Mr Zaki

Cooper, Rt Hon Frank Field MP, Lord Howard of Lympne, Mr Simon Olswang, Mrs Wendy Fidler, Mr John Reynolds, Mrs Ingrid Stellmacher, Most Rev. Peter Smith, Rt Revd David Gillett and Revd Malcolm Weisman (ex officio).

(Names are as given on the CCJ website on 30.7. 2012)

Chapter 12. At the Centre (2):Dedicated Staff

'Commitment to Truth and Reconciliation is a costly calling,without earthly reward.'
Graham Jenkins, a former Education Officer

Directors

There have been five Directors of CCJ during the last twenty years.

<u>Jim Richardson</u>

Canon Jim Richardson's interest in Christian-Jewish relations grew as Vicar of Leeds – which meant being 'Provost' to the city, where there is an influential and respected Jewish community. He became chairman of Leeds CCJ and of the Racial Harassment Commission set up by the Leeds Community Relations Council. He visited Israel as part of a high-level group that included the then Archbishop of York. From the beginning of his tenure as Director in 1988 Jim Richardson brought many gifts to CCJ and raised the profile of the organisation at a national level and greatly improved the quality of CCJ's publications, especially Common Ground. He developed a programme of informative visits to Israel to help church leaders become more aware of the actual situation. Under his leadership and thanks to the patient work of Paul Mendel, the number of local branches increased, including ones in universities, theological colleges and Anglican dioceses. He arranged for the visit of Cardinal Cassidy, who was President of the

Pontifical for Promoting Christian Unity, which is also responsible for the Vatican's relationship with the Jewish people to Britain as a guest of CCJ and played a large part in organising the 1991 Colloquium of International Council of Christians and Jews (ICCJ) at Southampton. Jim and Paul were also responsible for the launch at Lambeth Palace of a £1million appeal for CCJ and for a Reception at St James's Place in the presence of H M the Queen.

One difficulty for several directors, as it was for Jim, is that the job of director – unlike that of a vicar – did not come with a house. Commuting, as many people know, is tiring, especially the travelling home late at night after one of the many evening engagements that a director has to attend. Another difficulty was that when Jim took over the decision making process was unclear, so that at times a few officers took decisions without full consultation with the Executive Committee or even the director. Despite the difficulties, CCJ made real progress under Jim's leadership, but at the end of 1992 he decided the time was right for him to return to parochial ministry. His interest in CCJ continued and he gave outstanding leadership to Bournemouth CCJ, which regularly then and now has up to or over 100 people attending meetings. The Bishop of Winchester's invitation – arranged by Jim - to members of Bournemouth synagogue to tea at Wolvesey, the Bishop's home, which is adjacent to the ruins of the old palace, was greatly appreciated and reciprocated. In 2007 Jim Richardson was awarded an OBE for his services to the Church of England and particularly for his interfaith work.

Michael Latham

Michael Latham (soon to become Sir Michael Latham) was his successor – although for all too short a time. Michael had been a Conservative Member of Parliament from 1974 to 1992, and was an active member of the executive and a strong supporter of Israel. He had a wide range of contacts and helped to make CCJ's work better known. His many other interests and responsibilities, however, meant that at the end of the year, he resigned from this position, although he continued to give active support to CCJ.

Paul Mendel

Paul Mendel, with his wealth of experience was the obvious choice as Michael Latham's successor. Paul, the first Jew to be Director, had joined the staff of CCJ in the summer of 1985 as Assistant Director, following the sudden death of Leonard Goss. He brought to CCJ his wide experience of the business world and of work in the Jewish community. He soon became Deputy Director and combined his administrative skills with an ever-growing understanding of the varied and complex issues involved in Christian Jewish relations. At the end of 1998, Paul Mendel retired as Director, although he continued for a time to act as a consultant on fund-raising. The staff expressed their warm appreciation of his 'excellent leadership.' Paul, who had earlier been awarded an MBE, died early in 2011, when many tributes were paid to his work for CCJ and the Jewish community.

Margaret Shepherd

Sister Margaret Shepherd NDS, who had been on the staff of CCJ from 1989, first as Education Officer and then

Deputy Director, became the new Director – the first woman to do so. Margaret, a Roman Catholic, was a member of the Sisters of Sion, whose main 'charism' or divinely inspired gift is to promote dialogue between Christians and Jews. She entered the congregation as a trained teacher and taught English for several years. She then felt strongly called to the special work of the Congregation. She studied Rabbinics, full time, for three years at Leo Baeck College and then joined Sister Charlotte Klein and Sister Mary Kelly, pioneers in this field, at the Sister of Sion's Study Centre in London. Already at this stage she was involved with CCJ, but then in 1989 became CCJ's Education Officer. She brought to her work her deep respect and admiration for the Jewish people and Judaism, a deep knowledge of current Catholic thinking in this area, and her experience as a gifted teacher.

Even as Director, Sister Margaret Shepherd continued indefatigably to teach, lecture and write – as she still does. In a farewell tribute, when Sister Margaret left to become Provincial of the Sisters of Sion in the U.K., Eric Allen listed Margaret's many gifts: 'your spirituality as a nun, your academic studies, your time at Chepstow Villas and your time with us, writing, lecturing, broadcasting, and visiting all the local branches.' He expressed appreciation of her 'human touch' style of working and personal and pastoral interest in the individual members of CCJ. Eric Allen also acknowledged the personal cost of her work - 'standing in the middle, listening to both sides, being misunderstood and treated with hostility by both sides.'

David Gifford

Revd David Gifford became Chief Executive Officer in June 2006, following Sister Margaret Shepherd's retirement. David Gifford had joined the staff as Director of Development in January of that year.

David grew up in South Wales. He has a degree in geography from London University and a Master's degree in management from Sussex University. David has had a varied international career in education, marketing and communications, which as taken him to every continent. After several years in education, he went to the South Pacific Islands and taught at a local high school, whilst also tutoring in the philosophy of science for the University of the South Pacific in Suva, Fiji.

On his return to the UK, he worked for an international Christian charity specializing in leprosy. As Director of Fundraising, he achieved a big increase in its income. Next, David worked as a consultant for the International Red Cross in Geneva and then again in the South Pacific. He was then invited to head the European work of an international housing charity in USA and was promoted to its Director of International Development. Family needs necessitated a return once more to the UK and David became marketing director of a bioscience company. Music has also played a large part in David's life and he has sung in numerous choirs. More recently - with all his responsibilities at CCJ, CCJ David has also studied in Oxford for a degree in Theology was ordained as an Anglican clergyman (non-stipendary) in 2011.

David Gifford therefore, has brought very wide experience to his work as Chief Executive Officer of CCJ. He very quickly made himself aware of the many, often complex and sometimes controversial, issues involved in promoting good Jewish-Christian relations. Despite the enrichment that comes from deeper knowledge of other faiths and its adherents, David is clear that the distinctiveness of Judaism is very different from the distinctiveness of Christianity as a religion. Both communities should develop in a way that is right for them.

Under David's guidance CCJ's work has focussed on programmes, the effectiveness of which can be clearly evaluated. In 2010 the CCJ headquarters was moved to a smaller but more central and well-appointed office, at 21 Godliman Street, close to St Paul's Cathedral. The CCJ Iréne Rachel Library, which was opened in February 2010, is also located there. Besides ensuring that CCJ records are catalogued and made readily available, the Library has some 3,000 entries on Christian-Jewish dialogue. The library catalogue can be accessed on line and researchers and others who are interested are encouraged to visit the library.

The Team

All the directors have worked closely with other members of staff, who have been drawn from a wide range of Christian and Jewish traditions – itself evidence that people of faith can work together.

Canon Jim Richardson's team consisted of Paul Mendel as Deputy Director and Fr. Roger Clarke and then Sister

Margaret Shepherd as Education Officers, Mildred Goss as the indefatigable secretary and Barbara Hall as a charming and efficient Finance Officer. The beginning of 1992 saw the resignation of Mildred Goss as secretary. Her husband, Leonard, who had joined CCJ in 1950, became a staff member in 1975 and served the society faithfully until his sudden death in 1984. Mildred, always overworked, became a friend to many members of CCJ and had an unrivalled knowledge of the many issues with which the office is expected to deal.

Miss Erica Haigh, who had been Assistant Education Officer resigned at the end of 1995. Early in the next year, Ms Annagrette Mollers joined the staff on a part-time basis to help with research for *Common Ground* and with the Young Leaders Group. In June, Paul Mendel introduced the new secretary, Ms Frances Duke, and at the subsequent meeting Ms Fiona Gibbons as his Personal Assistant.

Sister Margaret Shepherd's team, described by Eric Allen as 'the best education team CCJ ever had' included Jane Clements and Revd Jonathan Gorsky, who like Sister Margaret continue, now in other positions, their devoted work to foster good Christian-Jewish relations.

Dr Jane Clements is an Anglican with wide experience in education. She first came across CCJ when she was about to teach a course on Judaism. She realised that despite her knowledge of Biblical studies and of the archaeology and history of the Near East, her knowledge of Judaism was purely academic. 'It seemed to me that my local CCJ might provide an excellent opportunity to engage with some practicalities – to meet those for whom Jewish tradition and liturgy was a living reality. In this I was not wrong.'

Jane has post-graduate qualifications in Hebrew and Jewish studies. She was Education Officer of CCJ and also became Deputy Director. Her particular field was Holocaust Education. On leaving CCJ, she founded The Forum for Discussion of Israel and Palestine (FODIP), which is a unique and timely initiative, seeking to promote and facilitate dialogue between Christians, Jews and Muslims in the UK on the Israeli/Palestinian conflict.

Revd Jonathan Gorsky is an Orthodox Jew. He trained as a historian and has great expertise in Jewish-Christian Relations, which he put to good use as Education Adviser. He now lectures at Heythrop College in the University of London.

Other members of the team were the Assistant Education Officer Rabbi Rachel Montagu, a Progressive Jew, who had been a congregational rabbi, before taking up lecturing posts at Birkbeck College, London. She continues her work as a teacher and was recently honoured with the award of the prestigious Leo Baeck College Rabbinic Fellowship. The Youth Officer was Gemma Abbs, who had degrees in theology and Middle East Politics. She had become involved in CCJ's Youth Section in 1999. Her place was taken by Louise Mitchell, who was a graduate of Cardiff University, where she had been active in the local CCJ. Mrs Elena Rowntree, who worked for CCJ for eighteen years with unfailing reliability and wide knowledge, was secretary and then Personal Assistant to the Chief Executive Officer. The Finance Officer was Mrs Gillian Taylor, who was succeeded by Mrs May Betts, and then by Ms Courage Edeko, who had a degree in Accountancy from the University of Benin, in Nigeria.

At first, Jane Clements and Elena Rowntree were members of David's team, before moving to new work or retiring. Sally Lorraine was General Adminstrator for four years. At the time of writing, Lindsay-Jane Butlin is the Administrator, Fiona Hulbert is Project Manager, the Finance Officer is Stephen Cutler, manages the work with local faith community leaders (Christian clergy and rabbis), Mr Rodney Curtis, a retired businessman, is the librarian. Vounteers and Interns also help with the work of CCJ.

(*Names are as given on the CCJ website on 30.7.2012*)

Chapter 13. 'The Souls of the Righteous are in the hand of God'

The dust returns to the earth as it was, and the soul returns to God who gave it.
Ecclesiastes 12, 7.

It is easy today to forget just how difficult and hard won has been the dramatic improvement in Christian-Jewish relations in the last seventy years. This progress is thanks to the creativity, openness, courage and tenacity of many men and women whose memory is cherished. Some have left a name behind them and it is right to report their praises. Those mentioned here are those whose death was recorded in *Common Ground*, but I know there are many others whose work and lives deserve equal if not greater appreciation - people who dared to hope that the misunderstandings of the past could be overcome and believed that Jews and Christians together have a message for humanity.

Many members will be grateful for the enriching friendships they have made through belonging to CCJ.

1991

1991 saw the death of Eva Koch Lawson and Mrs Betty Mandelson, who both had played a significant role in their local branches. Eva Koch Lawson, who died at the age of 90, had on *Kristallnacht* watched from her window a gang breaking up a nearby Jewish shop. The next day the Gestapo seized her husband. Eventually Eva's desperate efforts to leave Nazi Germany were successful, thanks to the Quakers. In Britain she was not allowed to work and once more it was the Quakers who helped her. After the war, she helped numerous German *au pair* girls and then in 1965 Eva was one of those who took the lead in establishing the Nottingham CCJ. She was a member of the committee from the start and was still an active member when she died. Mrs Betty Mandleson, 'a loving caring person,' was secretary of the Merseyside Branch and its first Life President.

1992

In 1992 two well-known supporters of CCJ died: Bishop Gerald Mahon and Viscountess Stansgate. Bishop Gerald Mahon had been an area bishop in the Roman Catholic diocese of Westminster. He was an active member of the CCJ Executive and Vice-Chairman. A scroll in his honour was given by CCJ to the Mill Hill Fathers. His place was taken by Bishop Charles Henderson. Viscountess Stansgate, who was the the first President of the Congregational Federation and a distinguished Vice-President of CCJ died late in 1991. At the suggestion of her son Tony Benn, a memorial lecture was given in her honour in July 1993 by Lord Jakobovits, who had recently retired from being Chief Rabbi. The lecture on 'Changing Patterns in Inter-human and Inter-faith relations' was also CCJ's contribution to the 1993 'Year of Interreligious Understanding and Co-operation.'

1993

1993 saw the death of the Venerable Witton-Davis, a former Archdeacon of Oxford, who was chairman of CCJ from 1958-1978 and thereafter a Vice President. In 1979 he was the first person to be awarded the Sir Sigmund Sternberg Award for a distinguished contribution to Christian-Jewish relations. He himself said that he knew of 'no organisation more worthy of support' than CCJ.

Three other faithful champions of CCJ also died in 1993: Revd Graham Jenkins, Lionel Slavid and Werner Mayer. Graham Jenkins, who was a Roman Catholic deacon, worked for several years at the bookshop at Westminster Cathedral. He joined CCJ in 1969 and in 1981 became organising secretary. Graham was a knowledgeable and persistent advocate of the new post-Vatican approach to Jews and Judaism. With the constant support of his wife Phyl, he led many pilgrimages to Israel. Lionel Slavid, on his retirement from the Inner London Education Authority, worked on a voluntary basis as an assistant educational officer. He was also a keen supporter of the Harrow branch. Werner Mayer was a well-known figure in Manchester. He was active in Manchester CCJ and played a leading role in creating the Jewish Museum, which is housed in the oldest surviving synagogue building in the city.

1996

1996 saw the death of Rabbi Hugo Gryn and several other much loved supporters of CCJ. Rabbi Hugo Gryn, a survivor of the Holocaust, was well known as the Rabbi of West London (Reform) synagogue and as a broadcaster. He was an outstanding interfaith activist. As well as serving on the CCJ Executive, he was a founder member of the Rainbow dialogue group, Vice-chair of the World Congress of Faiths and one of the first Co-chairs of Inter Faith Network for the UK Ernest Rea, Head of BBC religious broadcasting said that Hugo's 'journey was a Jewish journey.

But his humanity enabled him to talk to people of all faiths.' CCJ co-sponsored a memorial meeting attended by over 400 people – including the Chief Rabbi.

Other deaths in 1996 included Lord Finsberg, who was Hon.Treasurer, and Rabbi Bob Shafritz, Revd Sidney Black and Walter Sharman, who were all very supportive of their local branches, also died.

1997

The death in 1997 of Canon Roger Hooker, who had a long and distinguished career as an interfaith pioneer, was a sad and sudden blow to Birmingham CCJ. He died only four days after he had attended his first committee as Chair of the Birmingham CCJ. Roger Hooker never avoided difficult subjects, but thought they should be discussed with great sensitivity.

1997 also saw the death of Viscount Tonypandy, former speaker of the House of Commons, who took a personal interest in CCJ. It was said of him that 'He felt deeply about the Holocaust and was anxious to further the growing relationship between Christians and Jews. Often in his sermons he would speak with great gratitude of the Judaeo-Christian traditions.' Regret was also expressed at the death of Dr Jessel Hazelton, who had helped to found the Reading CCJ and served as secretary for several years.

1998

In 1998 many tributes were paid, on his death, to Edward Carpenter, who had been Dean of Westminster and a chairman of CCJ. As Harry Levy said, 'The memory of the righteous is a blessing. We have indeed been blessed by such a worthy and saintly life.' Christopher Anthony

Prendergarst, who held many public offices and was a conscientious Honorary Treasurer from 1991-1996, also passed away in 1998. Regret was also expressed at the deaths of Rabbi Bernard Hooker, a leading member of the Redbridge branch and of Mrs Joyce Howell, who had been active in the Hereford branch.

1999

The end of the century was marked by the passing away of two outstanding religious leaders, Cardinal Basil Hume and Lord Jakobovits, who had made an unforgettable contribution to the life of the nation.

Cardinal Basil Hume was a President of CCJ for twenty-three years. The Chief Rabbi, Jonathan Sacks, said of him, 'Cardinal Hume was a man of God because he was a man of the people… He turned strangers into friends.'

The death of Lord Jakobovits, a former Chief Rabbi and Joint President of CCJ, was also mourned. His son Joel said of him that his 'private and public *persona* were one and the same. The truth of the religious conviction and sense of social justice he carried within him was not subject to variance tailored to the occasion.' Lord Jakobovits was a keen supporter of Israel but bravely expressed concern 'for the inhuman conditions of thousands of Palestinians in wretched refugee camps' and recognised 'the justice of some Arab claims even when they conflict with ours.'

David Kessler, another firm supporter of CCJ, also died in 1999. David Kessler was responsible for making the *Jewish Chronicle* the most respected Jewish weekly in the world, which he achieved by dint of his unwavering desire for fairness – as CCJ has known to its benefit. He was passionately devoted to the cause of the Falasha black Jews and wrote an outstanding book, *The Falashas: the Forgotten Jews of Ethiopia.*

2000

2000 saw the death of two former Archbishops. Lord Runcie, who was Archbishop of Canterbury from 1980 to 1991 and a very supportive President of CCJ, was widely mourned. Lord Coggan, who was Archbishop of Canterbury, from 1974 to 1980, was Chairman of CCJ in the 80s and again became acting chairman for a year in 1992. An outstanding Hebrew and Biblical scholar, he gave long and devoted service to CCJ and to the International Council of Christians and Jews. CCJ also lost another very faithful member, Revd Dr Arthur Chadwick (1925-2000), a leading member of the Free Churches, who had been active in CCJ in Manchester and Hon. Treasurer of CCJ in the 1980s.

The death of Revd Richard Gutteridge was also mourned. He had been a strong supporter of Cambridge CCJ. His book *Open Thy Mouth for the Dumb* was a thorough study of woefully inadequate response of German Churches to Nazism. He often spoke to Christian clergy and the religious press on the subject of the Pharisees.

2003

The death in 2003 of Rabbi Dr Albert Friedlander was widely mourned. Albert Friedlander, who was Rabbi of the Westminster Synagogue, wrote extensively about the Holocaust, and was an active supporter of movements for peace and reconciliation. For some years he was chairman of the Week of Prayer for World Peace Committee. Tribute was also paid to Canon Brian Ettlinger for his long service to CCJ – especially as a faithful member of the Executive Committee - and to Sidney Sheridan for his invaluable help with *Common Ground*.

2005

In 2005, besides the death of Pope John Paul II and Simon Wiesenthal, several dedicated members of CCJ who had worked tirelessly for good relations between the faiths, also died. The death of Revd Dr Isaac Levy (better known as 'Harry') who was a life-long supporter of CCJ and who was for many years an Honorary Secretary and Editor of the journal was noted with much regret.

Two leading members of the London Society of Jews and Christians also died in 2005. Rabbi John Rayner - for many years rabbi of the St John's Wood Liberal synagogue and a guiding figure of the society and Professor Geoffrey Parrinder, who was a prolific author on world religions, was for a long time a President of the London Society of Jews and Christians.

2006

In 2006 the death of Bishop Charles Henderson, who was Vice-Chairman of CCJ from 1992 until his death in April 2006, came as a sad shock. He is remembered as a dedicated and tireless pastor. He also led the way in putting into practice the Second Vatican Council's documents on Christian unity and inter-faith dialogue. He served the Catholic Bishops' Conference of England and Wales as Chair of the Committee for Catholic Jewish Relations from 1992-2001, and also as Chair of the Committee for Other Faiths. Pope John Paul II recognised his expertise and knowledge in inter-faith dialogue by appointing him to the

Pontifical Council for Inter Religious Dialogue in 1990. His outstanding work over seventeen years in developing understanding and good relations between the Jewish and Catholic communities earned him, in 2001, the Interfaith Gold Medallion from the Sternberg Charitable Foundation. He was also a regular member of the Manor House Dialogue Group.

2009

2009 saw the death of Sidney Corob after a long illness. Sidney was passionate about the importance of interfaith relations, and was an energetic and generous vice-president of the Council of Christians and Jews and vice-chair of its executive committee from 1978-95. He helped fund study tours to Israel, enabling non-Jews of all backgrounds to gain a deeper understanding and appreciation of Israel's people, history and problems. In 1987 and 1990 he attended private audiences with the Pope.

2011

In March 2011 Paul Mendel - a former Director, who served CCJ loyally for many years - died after a long period of illness. Many tributes were paid to his work most especially the expansion of CCJ's educational work in schools and colleges as well as a marked growth in the number of branches in the regions. Later, in the same year many people gathered to mourn the death of Dr Seymour Spencer, who for many years was a leading member of the Oxford branch and regularly attended CCJ conferences.

Many other people, who were loyal members of CCJ, have not been named 'but their righteousness is not forgotten.'

Chapter 14. Together for the Future

God will judge between the nations
and arbitrate between many peoples.
They will hammer their swords into ploughshares
and their spears into sickles.
Nation will not lift sword against nation
No longer will they learn to make war.
Isaiah 2, 4

'We must advance from dialogue to a sense of joint-trusteeship. At the heart of the Jewish faith and of the Christian faith is the conviction that Jews and Christians alike have been recipients of divine truths, which are of immense importance.' These words, from Lord Coggan's sermon at CCJ's 50th Anniversary service at St Paul's Cathedral are a reminder that building trust between Jews and Christians is important, not just for members of the two religions, but for the future of humanity.

More recently, Lord Carey said 'CCJ is 'vital for our nation.' This work is extremely important for the health of our society and the nature of our democracy.' His words recall Archbishop William Temple's insistence in 1942 that the Council should deal 'with a problem of civilization and not only the relationship between Jew and Christian.' His view was echoed by Chief Rabbi Dr J H Hertz who said the central point was 'to consider the danger to civilisation involved in antisemitism.'

The formal resolution to establish the Council makes the same point. The introductory paragraph begins:

> 'That since the Nazi attack on Jewry has revealed that antisemitism is part of a general and comprehensive attack on Christianity and Judaism and on the ethical principles common to both religions which form the basis of the free national life of Great Britain...'

The public announcement went further and said:

> 'Nazi antisemitism, which is repugnant to the moral principles common to Christianity and Judaism alike, ... is not only a menace to the unity of every community in which it takes root, but it is the very negation of those values on which alone we believe that a new and better world can be established.'

CCJ also, in supporting the 'Three Faith Declaration' on post-war reconstruction, affirmed that 'there can be no permanent peace without a religious foundation.'

It is easy to forget Archbishop William Temple's warning that CCJ should not just deal with the relationship between Jew and Christian. Just as congregations of both synagogues and churches become preoccupied with their own affairs, so there is an ever present danger that dealing with the tensions between the Jewish and Christian communities will obscure this more important shared mission. These tensions, of course, need to be resolved and it is essential for Christians to repent of past hostility to Jews and to unlearn their prejudiced misunderstanding of that faith.

CCJ will need to continue to make sure that the memory of those who died in the Shoah is not forgotten nor the dangers of antisemitism and racism ignored. CCJ also needs to persevere in the vital task of providing accurate and balanced information to its members and to the public about the situation in Israel/Palestine and also continue to make known the work of the many groups in Israel/Palestine that are striving for a more just and peaceful future for that troubled area of the world. The importance of the study tours to Israel and the Yad Vashem seminars cannot be over-estimated.

CCJ also recognizes that there is an unfinished theological agenda in the dialogue of Jews and Christians. Several members of CCJ shared in the Manor House group, who together produced the ground-breaking book *Dialogue with a Difference* in 1992. Little new ground has been broken since then. Recently, CCJ has invited Rabbi Dr Tony Bayfield, who was a co-editor of *Dialogue with a Difference*, to convene a 'Theology Group,' which will, it is hoped produce a new book. The focus will be 'experiential or contextualised theology, namely a theology that addresses, even emerges out of, the day to day experience of practising Christians and Jews.' The intention, therefore, is rather different than academic theology. The discussions will take note of contemporary Western culture, where all faith groups are a minority, but also be aware of the legacy of history. The most challenging task will be to define the relationship 'in a way that is not a betrayal or empty relativism but which releases us from the insistence that ours is the only truth or better or preferred by God.'

Yet all this, as Lord Coggan said, is a preparation for joint-trusteeship of the divine truths that the two religions share.

Aggressive Secularism

Today the most dangerous threats to civilized society in Britain are not from Communism or Fascism, but from aggressive atheistic secularism and religious extremism. Banning a person from wearing a cross or saying a prayer with a patient may attract press attention, but the deeper issue, as several religious leaders have emphasised, is the attempt to exclude religious voices from public debate and to trample on the conscientious convictions of believers, for example, in the interest of gender equality.

The Archbishop of York, Dr John Sentamu, has said that Christianity is being wiped out from public life in the name of equality. The Archbishop of Canterbury, when he was asked about the Church's participation in public debate, replied 'The foot is still in the door, even if it is being squashed very painfully.' In 2011, the leader of the Catholic Church in Scotland, Cardinal Keith O'Brien, used his Easter message to attack 'aggressive secularism', saying that the enemies of Christianity want to 'take God from the public sphere'. The Chief Rabbi, Lord Sacks of Aldgate, has warned that Europe was dying because the growth of secularism.

The Challenges of Faith and Religious Leadership in Secular Society was also the subject in March 2011 for the Bilateral Commission of the delegations of the Chief Rabbinate of Israel and the Holy See's Commission for Religious Relations with the Jews at its tenth meeting. This suggests that while remembering the catastrophic events of the twentieth century, CCJ needs to devote as much attention to the current and future threats to a civilised society.

A New Approach

The new situation requires a fresh approach. The City Breakfast Seminars, which CCJ has recently started, are indicative of a new way in which leading members of the Christian and Jewish communities reflect together on current issues that face our society.

The first on Ethics and Capitalism attracted an audience of over 100 people. In the light of the recession, expenses scandals, bank bail-outs and excessive bonuses, the subject was highly topical. The speakers included Stephen Green, Chair of HSBC, Lord Levene of Lloyds and Lord Myners of HM Treasury. The second seminar was on 'The Place of Faith in Business.' In 2010 a seminar was held to reflect on the impact of the visit of Pope Benedict XVI to Britain. Speakers included Rabbi David Rosen and Lord Brennan, QC, who is President of the Catholic Union.

At another City Breakfast Seminar, hosted by Simmons and Simmons – a City of London law firm - John Micklethwaite, editor of *The Economist*, set the scene for an insightful analysis of 'Faith in Capitalism: how can we make the global economy more ethical?' There was an audience of almost 100 bankers, investment fund managers and lawyers. John Micklethwaite was ably followed by comments and observations by Lord Griffiths of Goldman Sachs, and Alex Brummer, City Editor of the *Daily Mail*. Overall, the speakers agreed that Faith brings challenges to capitalism but it is a two-edged sword. Capitalism, too, has things to say to Faith and questions some of the assumptions made in Judeo-Christian values. The event was chaired by Lord Justice Rix.

The City Breakfasts, which perhaps ought to be copied by some branches, reflect the determination of CCJ, in the Bishop of Manchester's words to the 2010 AGM, 'to engage intelligently and more visibly at every level with issues that are not only fundamental to our being, but also enable us to interpret our constitutional brief in a manner that preserves our integrity and keeps us more abreast with contemporary concerns of faith, culture and society.'

Religious Extremism

The danger of religious extremism in many faith communities means that CCJ's long struggle against antisemitism and all forms of religious discrimination remains a priority - especially as religion is by some people being used to justify acts of violence. This gives great importance to CCJ's work in universities, where small racist, antisemitic or Islamaphobic groups can cause trouble and distress to other students. Many chaplains and other staff members in Higher Education are likely to be grateful for the advice and support that CCJ can offer.

CCJ's work, therefore, is still vital because of the danger that extremism could tear the nation apart and that aggressive secularism wishes to exclude all religion from the public life of the nation. Moreover the major issues facing the world today, such as the poverty and marginalization of millions of people and the threats to the environment as well as the search for just and lasting peace are ones that call for the shared witness of Jews and Christians and of members of other faiths and all people of good will.

Unfinished Business

'While a huge amount has been accomplished by CCJ in its first seventy years there is much unfinished business, as the Revd David Gifford, the Chief Executive Office of CCJ has said:

> 'The world changes. Broadly it will be unlikely for us to hear voices from Christian pulpits accusing the Jews of 'deicide.' There will be few rallying calls for conversionary activity aimed at the Jewish people. A broader call for the building of relationships is more likely to be heard as well as a sadder and deeper reflection of Christian complicity in the *Shoah*.
>
> Initiatives like Holocaust Memorial Day, in which CCJ, with its partner, CTBI, plays a proactive part, ensures the lessons of the Holocaust do not slip from Christian memory and continue to play their part in any theological reflection of Christian relationship with Jews. They need not dominate and define that relationship but it must be there.
>
> Jews and Christians have unfinished business; we must allow ourselves the space and honesty to embrace the reality that we probably always will. The person of Jesus; our troubled and painful history; our witness to a secular world, a prophetic call to a crowded planet and society motivated by greed, self-interest and the survival of the fittest, and a misunderstanding of what exactly Christians and Jews believe, are just some of the issues we need to grapple with, in a spirit of understanding and with courage.

The good news is, as we move on, that many of us have built, over the decades, deep respectful relationships with each other. This is the seed bed in which our trust of one another may flourish. The more challenging news is that this needs constantly to be replenished with fresh energy, renewed commitment and a rejection of an easy complacency that all is now well and so always will be.'

Of course, no one can foresee the future. CCJ has always had to respond to a changing situation as well as being alert to unexpected events that can cause strains between Jews and Christians.

This good relationship, however, is of value, not only to members of the two religions, but for society as a whole. As Chief Rabbi, Dr J H Hertz said when CCJ was founded, 'National life and religion, civilization all depend on the attitude of any society to the Jew.' Jews and Christians are joint trustees of the moral and ethical teaching which remains the foundation on which just and harmonious community life has to be built. In Lord Coggan's words, 'We are partners. We are co-trustees. Come, let us go - and go together for the future.'

* * *

Marcus Braybrooke

Marcus Braybrooke is a retired parish priest, who has been active in interfaith work for many years. He author of over forty books. Marcus is married to Mary, who is a retired social worker and a magistrate and who has shared in the parochial ministry and the interfaith work. They have a son and a daughter and six granddaughters and a poodle, Toffee.

Marcus Braybrooke has ministered in Highgate in London; Frindsbury in Kent; in Swainswick, Wells and Bath in Somerset; and in the Baldons in Oxfordshire.

After gaining a degree in history and theology at Cambridge, Marcus studied for a year at Madras Christian College and then at Wells Theological College. He has studied in Jerusalem and has led many pilgrimages to the Holy Land. He was Director of the Council of Christians and Jews from 1984-7. He has written several books about Judaism and Jewish Christian Relations. Marcus Braybrooke is President of the World Congress of Faiths and a Co-Founder of the Three Faiths Forum..

In 2004 he was awarded a Lambeth degree by the Archbishop of Canterbury 'in recognition of his contribution to the development of inter-religious co-operation and understanding throughout the world.' He is also a recipient of Sir Sigmund Sternberg Interfaith Gold Medallion and the Kashi Ashram Life-time Service Award.

Books by Marcus Braybrooke

Together to the Truth 1971

The Undiscovered Christ of Hinduism 1973

Interfaith worship 1974

Time to Meet 1990

Wide Embracing Love 1990

Children of One God: A History of the Council of Christians and Jews 1991

Pilgrimage of Hope: One Hundred Years of Global Interfaith Dialogue 1992

Stepping Stones to a Global Ethic 1992

Be Reconciled 1992

Dialogue with a Difference (Ed with Tony Bayfield), 1992

Love without Limit 1995

Faith in a Global Age 1995

How to Understand Judaism 1995

A Wider Vision: the World Congress of Faiths 1996

The Wisdom of Jesus, 1997

The Miracles of Jesus (with James Harpar), 1997

All in Good Faith (Ed with Jean Potter), 1997

The Explorers' Guide to Christianity 1998

Testing the Global Ethic (Ed with Peggy Morgan), 1998

Christian-Jewish Dialogue: the Next Steps 2000

Learn to Pray 2001

Bridge of Stars (Ed) 2001

What we can learn from Hinduism 2002

What we can learn from Islam 2002

Lifelines (Ed) 2002

One Thousand World Prayers 2003

365 Meditations for a Peaceful Heart and World 2004

Sustaining the Common Good (with Kamran Mofid) 2005

A Heart for the World: the Interfaith Alternative 2006

365 Meditations and Inspirations on Love and Peace 2006

Interfaith Witness in a Changing World 2007

Prayers and Blessings (Ed) 2007

Beacons of the Light: 100 holy people who have shaped the Spiritual History of Humanity 2009

Meeting Jews 2010

E-books by Marcus Braybrooke,

Hinduism: a Christian Reflection,
Islam; a Christian Reflection,
Peace in Our Hearts, Peace in Our World: A practical interfaith daily guide to a spiritual way of life.
Christians and Jews Building Bridges
available from www.lulu.com
Widening Vision: The World Congress of Faiths and the Growing Interfaith Movement
Available from www.amazon.co.uk – kindle

Acknowledgements

There are many people to thank. First, of course, the members of CCJ, of whom, sadly, only a few are named. Without their enthusiasm and commitment there would be no story to tell. I am particularly grateful to those who supplied information or who have read and advised on the text: Zaki Cooper, Canon Jim Richardson, Sr Margaret Shepherd, Jonathan Gorsky, Dr Jane Clements, Rabbi Tony Bayfield. Lord Harries, Brian Pearce, Ruth Weyl and the Revd Eric Allen. I am also very grateful to the Revd David Gifford, the Chief Executive Officer, of the Council of Christians and Jews for suggesting I wrote the book and his advice and help and for allowing me access to the minutes of the meetings of the Trustees. I did not, however, see any of the Council's files and correspondence. Opinions expressed are, of course, my own and may not reflect the views of the CCJ Trustees. Mistakes are also my responsibility. Once again, I am very grateful to my wife Mary, for her encouragement and patience as I kept checking and revising the text. We joined the CCJ over forty years ago and have rich memories of many friendships.

The words on the title page are from the song 'Bridge over troubled water' by Simon and Garfunkel ©.

I often think of prejudice and antisemitism as like weeds in the garden. You think you have rooted out the weeds, but go away for a week, and they are back. We need, in Shakespeare's words to be 'as vigilant as a cat to steal the cream.' Even more important, may we work and pray together for that day when 'the sun of righteousness will rise with healing in its wings.'

Marcus Braybrooke 31 July 2012